Middle Age

THE ART OF LIVING SERIES
Series Editor: Mark Vernon

From Plato to Bertrand Russell philosophers have engaged wide audiences on matters of life and death. *The Art of Living* series aims to open up philosophy's riches to a wider public once again. Taking its lead from the concerns of the ancient Greek philosophers, the series asks the question "How should we live?". Authors draw on their own personal reflections to write philosophy that seeks to enrich, stimulate and challenge the reader's thoughts about their own life.

Published
Clothes   *John Harvey*
Death   *Todd May*
Deception   *Ziyad Marar*
Fame   *Mark Rowlands*
Hunger   *Raymond Tallis*
Illness   *Havi Carel*
Me   *Mel Thompson*
Middle Age   *Christopher Hamilton*
Pets   *Erica Fudge*
Sport   *Colin McGinn*
Wellbeing   *Mark Vernon*
Work   *Lars Svendsen*

Forthcoming
Faith   *Theo Hobson*
Money   *Eric Lonergan*
Sex   *Seiriol Morgan*
Science   *Steve Fuller*

Middle Age

Christopher Hamilton

ACUMEN

First published in 2009 by Acumen

Acumen Publishing Limited
Stocksfield Hall
Stocksfield
NE43 7TN
www.acumenpublishing.co.uk

ISBN: 978-1-84465-165-8

British Library Cataloguing-in-Publication Data
A catalogue record for this book is available
from the British Library.

Extracts from Philip Larkin, "I Have Started to Say" and "Maiden Name", from
Collected Poems, and "This Be The Verse", from *High Windows*, are reprinted with
permission, Faber and Faber Ltd/© The Estate of Philip Larkin. Extracts from
T. S. Eliot, "East Coker", from *Collected Poems 1909–1962*, are reprinted with
permission, Faber and Faber Ltd/© The Estate of T. S. Eliot.

Typeset in Warnock Pro.
Printed in the UK by the MPG Books Group.

In memory of K.

With yellow pears hangs
And full of wild roses
The land into the lake,
You gracious swans,
And drunk with kisses
You dip your heads
Into the hallowed-sober water.

But oh, where shall I find
When winter comes, the flowers, and where
The sunshine
And shade of the earth?
The walls stand
Speechless and cold, in the wind
Weathercocks clatter.

Friedrich Hölderlin, "The Middle of Life"

Contents

The following, apart from "Preface", "Afterword" and "A final thought" are not chapter headings, but rather should be seen as themes or signposts around which thoughts are grouped for a stretch of the discussion. They do not always correspond to moments where reflection breaks off in the text.

Preface

This book represents an attempt to think through some of the central features of middle age from a philosophical perspective. I have drawn throughout on my own experiences in order to make sense of the phenomenon – or, rather, phenomena – that constitute middle age. At the core of these experiences was one event that changed my life forever: in a single moment my life was turned inside out and I was left having to rethink just about everything that was important to me. Nothing looks to me now as it once did, and this book forms part of my attempt to make sense of how it all looks now, and how it used to look.

Because I have drawn on the experiences of my own life in order to write this book, it may well be that it contains passages that suggest a contradictory or conflicted account of middle age. I have not sought to smooth out any of these discrepancies, and I am not disturbed by their presence in a work of philosophy. The only point in seeking to erase them would be in order to try to show that life is less contradictory or conflicted than it actually is.

My reflections here can make no claim to completeness, and I have not had any kind of ambition for such finality in mind in working on them. Moreover, although I have tried to connect my experiences of middle age with those of others, it is inevitable that some of what I say will seem on occasion to be in some ways highly particular to me. This would only be a failure if I had the absurd ambition to speak for others, to answer their questions about middle age for them. But any writing worth reading leaves spaces for the readers' thoughts and does not seek to say everything on the topic with which it deals. It is true that philosophy, at least in its academic guise, often has the ambition to say everything that could be said on the topics with which it deals. But that is not my view of the subject, not least because there seems to me to be a lack of generosity in such ambition. It is more than sufficient if one says enough to help readers to think their own thoughts in a more productive or deeper way. The point of philosophy, as I understand it, is, among other things, to enable one to experience life more fully and with a greater intensity, and my aim in this book has been to do something that might help anyone who has an interest in the topics it explores to find his or her way to a fuller response to life.

A note on references

This book contains no footnotes. I have indicated the source of quotations by giving in parentheses the book or essay title from which the quotation is taken, together with the page number of the edition in question. Where a quotation has come from an internet source, I have given no page number, but the relevant passage will nonetheless be easy to locate. Translations are mine except where indicated.

Acknowledgements

I am indebted to many people and I am very grateful to them all: Harry Chapman, whose conversation is a source of such pleasure and who made a suggestion about the first line; Laurent Disdier for knowing what it is like; Sebastian Gardner, who has given me so much over the years; Steven Gerrard for supporting the project from the beginning; Tabea Kretschmann for many suggestions on improving the text, for her intellectual depth, and for her fine sensibility; Michael Newton, without whose wisdom and friendship I would have been lost; Clemens Sedmak, who has given me much encouragement; Edith Steffen for her unfailing kindness; Jonathan Steffen for his generous hospitality; Max Storey, whose sense of the ridiculous has brightened so many evenings; Susannah Ticciati for being such a good friend and colleague; Mark Vernon for inviting me to write this book and responding so positively to it; Jason Whiston for his irony and ability to laugh; and Kate Williams for her careful copy-editing.

The only thing that should surprise us is that there are still
some things that can surprise us
                              La Rochefoucauld (*Maximes*, 384)

Most people enter into middle age gradually; I was thrown into it
in a moment.

About six years ago, when I was thirty-eight, one of my brothers
told me that the man I had taken to be my father all my life, and
who died when I was eighteen, was not my father. My real father
was not K, but H. H is still alive. He is eighty-five, and almost blind
and deaf.

I have four older siblings and one younger. What I was told when
I was thirty-eight was that my four older siblings had known most
of my life that my real father was H, as, indeed, had K. K never
wanted me to know, and my older siblings acquiesced in this,
believing it to be for the best. H was a teacher in a local Catholic
primary school, and my mother came to know him because two of
my older brothers went to that school. She met him at a parents'
evening. He was already married, and had three children with his
wife, with whom he still lived; that family played a large role in
the local Catholic community. He also lived close to my mother
and the two families knew each other: H's children and my older
Hamilton siblings were on friendly terms. My mother and H began
an affair that lasted two to three years: she says three, he says two.

1

Their meetings were mainly furtive assignations. I was deliberately conceived when K found out about the affair and confronted first my mother and then H. My mother claimed to K that she was already pregnant when he found out what was going on, but this was untrue: she decided to conceive a child precisely because the affair was now exposed and at an end.

My mother and K divorced when I was nine. Their marriage had been in a state of collapse for years. K moved away; I saw him about once a month. He always treated me as his own son.

When I was old enough, I was sent to the school where H taught. I was thus partly educated in the classroom, with thirty-odd other children, by the man who was my real father, although neither he nor I knew this fact. He made a strong impression on me as a teacher, and on three or four occasions during my teaching career, and before I found out about his relation to me, I thought of him and was aware that my teaching style was rather similar to his. I took this to be a coincidence and nothing else. I even once told some students of mine an anecdote about him, having no idea that I was speaking about my father.

I was profoundly disturbed by what I was told. A problematic period typical of middle age, which had in any case been preparing itself in me for a year or two, was brought in a moment to the surface, and I was precipitated into a deep re-evaluation and reassessment of all that I am – for I am no longer who I was. In one sense, my life has been broken in two by my new knowledge: it has at one and the same time changed everything and yet left everything as it was; it has also distanced me from my childhood and early years, yet brought them back to me with the full force of a living reality. If I made a transition into middle age that for others takes longer, then this casts an especially bright light on it.

***

Among the many purposes the family has, explicitly or otherwise, is to conceal from us the radical contingency of our lives. It is simply a matter of chance that we are born to the parents we have, into a given family, community, socioeconomic group or class, speaking a particular mother tongue, with a certain history and cultural inheritance. It is also a matter of luck that we are born male or female, good-looking or otherwise, physically strong or weak, and with certain (latent) talents, abilities, aptitudes and so on. None of this is chosen, and we know this to be true. But the thought is in some ways unbearable, especially, perhaps, in an age in which we place so much value on choice. The philosopher Herbert Fingarette describes it thus:

> There is a certain eerie feeling when I think about the amazing accident that I was born into life. It's much the same eerie feeling I have when thinking of the trivial changes of circumstance that could have meant my wife might never have been, or that my daughter, the daughter I actually have and love, might never have come to be. I reflect on the utterly accidental nature of our existence, on the unplannable, uncontrollable, unpredictable character of the fact that there happen to exist these particular individuals and not others, that in the course of our life we have run into these particular life situations rather than any of the infinitely many variations on them that might have come to be. Appreciating this, I appreciate how little that is fundamental in my life and my world has been in my power.   (*Death*, 35–6)

But parents' love for their children and the cultural inheritance they seek to pass on to them – if they do – work to conceal what we know, and to reassure each of us that *I* am the one that was wanted when this man and this woman sought to have a child. Those people who know that they are "an accident" feel in a small way, perhaps, a certain mild discomfort at that thought, but if they are loved by their parents it is usually no more than that. Yet they are vaguely sensing something that is a truth most of us find disagreeable.

This sense of the arbitrariness of our coming to be comes out wonderfully in the figure of Levin and his reactions to the birth of his son in *Anna Karenina*. Just after the birth, he hears the baby crying. Tolstoy writes:

> It was a bold, insolent voice that had no consideration for anything, it was the cry of the new human being who had so incomprehensibly appeared from some unknown realm ... Whence and why had he come? Who was he? ... He [Levin] could not at all accustom himself to the idea. It seemed something superfluous, something overflowing, and for a long time he was unable to get used to it. (*Anna Karenina*, 710)

Evidently we are dealing with a mystery that is not at all cleared up by recounting the facts of human reproduction. It is a mystery that attends our very sense of what human life is, gives something of the form to that life as we are familiar with it. And it is striking that Levin's sense of the mystery here is only heightened by his incapacity to feel any love for his son: he feels, Tolstoy writes, merely repulsion before, and pity towards, the baby. Later Kitty, Levin's wife, and the baby are caught in a thunderstorm, during which Levin fears for their safety. At this moment, love for the baby begins to arise in him, and he is relieved to find that this is so.

Levin's sense of the baby is contained by his growing love for him. This does not mean that he no longer sees a mystery in the birth of his son. The thought is rather that the mystery is something that he can take pleasure and joy in – Tolstoy makes this clear – and, in doing so, it means that his answer to the question about his baby "Who is he?" is given by the love he now feels. In a sense one might say that the answer simply *is* that he loves him. But this is, so to speak, less an answer than a way of living with there being no answer. For, in loving his son, Levin finds himself loving *this* human being, and in loving *this* human being he *places* the question about who he, the baby, is; he makes clear why it cannot be answered except by pointing to his love for him. The love strips the contingency from the fact that it is sheer chance that this baby is born to him by allowing him to think and feel that it is *this* baby that is born to him, and no other. There is now, for Levin, in his love, no other baby he could have had, and that is his answer, which is a non-answer, to the question "Who is he?".

Levin's love is connected with the intense physical presence of the baby: it is profoundly focused on the baby's body. It is in tenderness for his fragile physical being that such love finds its true spiritual home. Accordingly, Levin's love for his baby begins to grow when he fears for his physical safety. A friend of mine with two young children remarked to me once, when the older child, a boy, was about three years old, that she had seen since his birth how *affectionate* people are, and there certainly is something about the physical being of a child that *naturally* calls forth this response in people: the desire to touch and caress. Another friend of mine, sitting with her baby on her lap, turned to her husband and exclaimed, "I could *eat* him!" I sometimes wonder if adult human beings would ever be genuinely tender to one another if we did not have the natural life cycle of birth, growth and death that we do have: if, that is, we and those around us never had been children. Creatures otherwise like us but born as adults might simply not evoke in one another the tenderness that two adults can inspire in each other.

There is, I am suggesting, something redemptive in a parent's love for a child: redemptive of the contingency of the child's being, and redemptive of his or her body. In this love the child is redeemed from being just some child or other, some chance creature, as it were, and becomes this unique, irreplaceable human being. Human life would probably be unliveable – and it would certainly be a great deal bleaker – without this love. Love, from this point of view, does not reveal who the child really is in his or her contingency. Rather, it creates something – a sense of who and what we are – that makes life bearable. This is one of those places where we see the necessity of a certain kind of illusion to find a purpose and meaning in our lives. But it is a completely natural illusion, because the love parents have for their children is a *natural* feature of human beings' psychology and spiritual condition.

A child grows into his parents' love, taking it not merely for granted, but as his right. As he does so, his character develops and he gradually becomes aware of the kinds of personality traits he has, if only implicitly and inchoately aware. But, in being loved, those character traits are accepted by those around him – that is part of what it means for parents to love their child – and the contingency of his being thus and so does not strike him. At any rate, for most that is something of an ideal of the relations between parent and child.

For most people, this sense of things fractures when the question "Who am I?" first arises with an insistent voice in that period of life we call adolescence, and it is significant that it is then that parents' love comes to seem insufficient to a young person and a need is felt for other kinds of love: the love of friends and the excitement of erotic love, newly sensed. The second period when this question is likely to arise is in middle age, when the issue of one's identity becomes pressing once again.

When I was told about H, my first overwhelming sense of myself was as if I were polluted by something foreign. I felt as if my flesh and blood were literally composed of something alien to me, something that I did not know but which was inside me and composed me. I felt as if I wanted to vomit it out and whenever I went running at that time – I run about five miles, three times a week – I felt as if I were purging or punishing my body. I have no idea how typical such a deeply corporeal response is to the kind of knowledge I had gained; it may be that others in a similar situation do not have that feeling about themselves much, or at all. I think it was fairly predictable for me, however, since a sense of the body and its powers to pollute and be polluted has been with me most of my life. My body has often seemed to me to be something that, as it were, lies in wait for me in order to entrap me or subvert me. I have, for example, sometimes found it hard to escape from the sense that sexual desire and sexual activity are polluting; and for very long periods in my life I have not been able to sleep at night with a sense that my body and I are at peace with one another.

In an interesting essay, Virginia Woolf complained that:

> with a few exceptions ... literature does its best to maintain that its concern is with the mind; that the body is a sheet of plain glass through which the soul looks straight and clear, and, save for one or two passions such as desire and greed, is null, and negligible and non-existent.   (*On Being Ill*, 4)

The situation has in many respects changed in literature since Woolf wrote, but it has not in philosophy, which still has, in general, a very poor understanding of the body. Be that as it may, Woolf goes on:

> On the contrary, the very opposite is true. All day, all night the body intervenes; blunts or sharpens, colours or discolours, turns to wax in the warmth of June, hardens to tallow in the murk of February. The creature can only gaze through the pane – smudged or rosy; it cannot separate off from the body like the sheath of a knife or the pod of a pea for a single instant; it must go through the whole unending process of changes, heat and cold, comfort and discomfort, hunger and satisfaction, health and illness ...   (*Ibid.*, 4–5)

In these terms, I could say that my sense of my body as polluted was a sense of its immense, heavy, compromising, opaque presence to me, *as* me: as Woolf indicates, like tallow or wax.

And this understanding of my body as polluted was, in part at least, an increased sense of my mortality: of my death, or just of death. In fact, for cultures in which issues of ritual pollution play a large role, such as ancient Greek culture, death itself is considered polluting: there were all kinds of prohibitions and injunctions surrounding the treatment of the corpse, contact with which was considered defiling and thus needed to be regulated in various ways. It is unclear why death was considered polluting, but it may have something to do with the idea that, in death, a human being is totally vanquished by his or her body: all the labour of culture, a large part of which goes into the effort to invest the corporeal side of our life with meaning – think here of the elaborations, prohibitions, directives and so on that surround such activities as eating, sleeping, defecating, having sex, washing and so on – is here rendered null and void. The corpse represents, as it were, the complete failure of this labour of culture: it lies there inert, a sign, so to speak, of the failure of human beings to be anything other than animals. Yet it is also uncanny: faced with a corpse one has the sense that this cannot be a dead person, that he or she must surely be able to get up and walk. Wittgenstein remarked that the human body is the best picture of the human soul (*Philosophical Investigations* II, iv, 178), and this point applies here: the dead body looks for all the world as if it must still be ensouled, still animate, and thus not really be a *dead* body at all – just sleeping, perhaps, or resting. This can be so even when the body is badly mutilated. In the film adaptation of Ian McEwan's novel *Enduring Love*, after John Logan has fallen from the balloon, Jed and Joe approach the body. It is horrifically injured, collapsed like a concertina, with Logan's guts spilled out over the ground and with blood issuing from the mouth. Jed asks Joe, "Do you think he's dead?", a question that must seem superfluous if any does, yet Joe later says, "In a funny way, I knew what he meant, because I kept on expecting him to get up, walk away...". There is something unbelievable in the sight of a dead body: unbelievable in the thought that this really is death for that person.

So it is, perhaps, hardly surprising after all that death – the dead body – has been felt to be polluting. When I felt my body to be polluted, and when others in middle age become increasingly aware of their mortality as their body starts to age in a way that cannot be ignored, there is felt the cold presence of death. In a sense, when I wanted to vomit up the pollution I felt to be in me, I wanted to vomit up my own mortality, not least because I felt myself to be totally out of control of my own body and its functions, just as I shall be when I do die. I had a feeling that not merely was this man, H, my former teacher, literally inside me, but so was the whole line of his family: parents, grandparents and so on. I had – I still have – little idea what I was carrying around with me, in me.

It is, in fact, probably in an increased sense of death, of one's own mortality, that one first grasps the significance of middle age. This has a corporeal side, but it is also connected with the idea that time is running out.

The corporeal side of this process manifests itself in profound changes in the body. My sense of being polluted when I found out about H may have been intense, but I think it was simply a heightened form of an experience of the body that attends middle age. For in mid-life one's body suddenly makes its presence more and more felt. This can often be so in an unpleasant manner. Some people in middle age, for example, are acutely aware of becoming increasingly physically weaker. In this, the body shows itself to be profoundly vulnerable to natural processes over which it has little or no control, or, as one might put it, shows itself to *be* a natural process over which one has little or no control. Perhaps this touches women more than men, at least generally, in that they have to cope with the menopause. But for both men and women there is a sense, I think, that the body is being reclaimed by nature, that nature is asserting its rights over the body, and that the grave is already pulling one down. Of John Webster's preoccupation with death, T. S. Eliot wrote that he "saw the skull beneath the skin" ("Whispers of Immortality", in his *Collected Poems*). This is something that can be said of all of us in the experience of middle age: the skull starts to stare out at us as we look in the mirror, or as we look at photographs of ourselves when we were younger and suddenly see the change in appearance. It is, in fact, as if death is already inside one, and one knows one can do nothing to rid oneself of it.

Rainer Maria Rilke gave expression to this sense of death in his *The Notebooks of Malte Laurids Brigge*. The protagonist is living in Paris, and feels he is surrounded by death. He writes:

> And when I think of those ... whom I have seen or of whom I have heard: it's always the same. They had their own death. There are men who carry it around in their armour, inside, like a prisoner; then there are women who grew very old and small and then passed away discreetly and grandly on an enormous bed, as if on a stage, in front of the whole family, the servants and the dogs. The children too, even the really small ones, had their own child's death: they pulled all their energies together and died a death which they already were and which they would have become.
>
> (*Die Aufzeichnungen des Malte Laurids Brigge*, 18)

Rilke's point, I take it, is that the very being of a person's life is something he or she will express in dying. This being is, looked at from one perspective, something corporeal. It manifests itself in a person's characteristic ways of moving, gesturing, walking, smiling and so on. And in middle age many become aware, perhaps, or more aware, of their very being manifested in, incorporated in, the body: in its typical forms of awkwardness, recalcitrance, energy, demands and so on. In that sense, a person's death is there with him in his body, giving contour and form to the kinds of things that his body can do for him, or that his body is for him.

In a way, the heightened feeling of the body in mid-life involves a partial eclipse of the outer world, as does any acute awareness of the body. Part of physical ageing is that the world becomes increasingly abstract or weightless, both in terms of its material presence and in terms of one's projects, goals and ambitions, that is, that the consciousness of the body begins to eclipse the consciousnesses of the world. This does not, or need not, mean that one ceases to care about the world without, but it means that that world, including those parts of it that are one's aims and purposes, can increasingly come to seem an object, or a fit object, of anecdote or caricature. At any rate, that is how I started to experience my own life. When I once said to a friend that I sometimes find Charles Dickens irritating because his characters are so often caricatures, he replied that this is precisely why Dickens is one of his favourite authors: Dickens sees how we all become caricatures of ourselves as we get older. I now understand why my friend said this.

This situation, in which the world seemed to become for me somewhat weightless, is a dimmer version of the fact that when one is in physical pain, nothing exists but one's own body. The world starts to lose its claims on one as the body moves into the centre of one's consciousness. Hence, the circle of my concerns in some way seemed to shrink, which meant I felt in many ways isolated from those around me, and they, in turn, felt shut out from me. This was one reason why they often could not help me: they had, in a way, begun to exist less for me, to have less reality. Just as a persistent headache means that one's attention to others is compromised, so too my persistent sense of defilement in my body meant that my attention to others was compromised. Some of them took this as a rejection of them. It was, however, not an explicit rejection, but simply the dark side of the bright light that was burning so fiercely in my consciousness of, and in, my body.

However, there can be another side to the body in middle age. For, despite the deeply problematic nature of my body for me in the light of what I now know about H, and despite the fact that I do sometimes experience my body as caught up in a process of decay, I also have a sense – and this is one of the benefits of middle age that many experience – of increased power or potency of the body. Middle age may be a time that brings much with which we have to cope or come to terms, but it can also offer liberation from some of the acute physical awkwardnesses of earlier phases of life. In a way, middle age is as problematic as it is precisely because it holds within itself two faces: the face turned towards death, and the face turned towards potent life and energy. This may be one reason why, for example, Friedrich Nietzsche, who is one of the few philosophers who have really worried about middle age – indeed, about the phases of life as such – conceptualized his own middle age as being a kind of ripe autumnal fruit: such fruit has had, as Keats so magnificently celebrated in his "To Autumn", all the summer sun poured into it and is thus in a state of extraordinary plenitude; yet it has but a short time in this condition before it must rot.

The way in which death is more acutely present for people in middle age is also, as I have already noted, a matter of sensing that time is running out, not least because time seems to be going so much faster. This can be so in terms of thinking that there is much one would like to do but will not because there simply is too little time left to do it. But I think there is another sense of this: in middle age one grasps that one has a certain character or personality – that one *is* this kind of person – and that this was never chosen or willed. I have an especially acute sense of this, since, for example, I became a teacher of philosophy, German and French, and H was a teacher – of French. Moreover, two of his three children by his wife are teachers. And I see also temperamental similarities between H and me. More generally, the combination of whatever we were at birth and of our experiences will have turned us into something largely unforeseen and probably undesired: most of us are likely to find out that we are not what we wanted to be or imagined we were. Hence, this experience is usually extremely painful. In my view, it is central to morality that we cope – that we each learn to cope – with being who we are, partly because doing so can have important and far-reaching effects on lovers, friends and so on, but also because being able to cope with what we have become is key to being able to find much by way of sense or meaning in life; if a person turns out to be permanently faced or threatened by a character that he cannot fathom or grasp then this is likely to lead to a feeling of rupture, confusion or disorder. But we each also know that whatever the struggles here, we will never be what we want to be, or feel we ought to be, and the sense of time's running out, and thus of death, is thus a sense of being, as it were, condemned to existing as this person and no other.

In her story "The Thirtieth Year", Ingeborg Bachmann brings out some of these aspects of middle age:

> He had seen so many possibilities for himself, had thought, for example, that he could become anything: A great man, a pioneer, a philosophical light ... Or an energetic man of action ... Or a revolutionary ... Or an idler in wisdom ...
>
> Never for one moment had he feared that the curtain could open ... as it did now ... and he would receive his cue, and that he would have to show what he really thought and was able to do; that he would have to make clear what really mattered to him. Never had he thought that from a thousand and one possibilities a thousand had been squandered and missed – or that he had had to miss them, because only one of them was really his.
>
> He knows now that he too is in the trap.
>
> ("Das dreißigste Jahr", 17–19)

And the uncanny oddity of the kind of experience I am discussing is that one can feel that numerous possibilities are still open even as one carefully works a way into just a single possibility. I have expended virtually all my creative and intellectual energy and abilities, such as they are, into becoming a philosopher, but only when I reached middle age did I realize that this possibility, which had become a reality, means that I have missed or squandered other opportunities. Somehow or other I preserved myself in the thought that, even as this was the only possibility I was seeking to realize, the others were not really cast aside: they lay there, and could be taken up and activated. But this is not so: I *am* this.

This experience is, I think, two-sided, and the two sides look, or feel, as if they are in conflict with each other. On the one hand, one could feel a sense of the extreme *weight* of who one is and what one has done, a sense of its fixity and inevitability. An aspect of this is well brought out by J. P. Stern in a discussion of Schopenhauer:

> Our lives are, after all, at best like a good novel, in which during our first reading, each new event had kept us in suspense by its unexpectedness, yet looking back on the whole we are at last struck by the necessity (the agreement between events and fully formed expectations) of each episode, by the unfreedom of each previously "free" choice.   (*Re-Interpretations*, 181)

Coming to terms with who one is involves struggling with recalcitrant and stubborn traits of character. Looking at this process in retrospect delivers a sense of inevitability of the kind Stern describes. Yet, on the other hand, this very sense of weight and inevitability, looked at as now past, gives rise to, or is, a certain dreamlike quality, precisely because the notion of choice seems to have evaporated, leaving one's life as something that *happened* to one. In this dreamlike sense of things, one's life seems peculiarly unreal or insubstantial, strangely *light*. In his autobiography *The*

Summing Up, Somerset Maugham – a much underrated writer, in my view – brings this out well:

> I have never quite lost the sense that my ... life was a mirage ... which, even while I was playing my part in it, I could look at from a distance and know for the mirage it was. When I look back on my life, with its successes and failures, its endless errors, its deceptions and its fulfilments, its joys and its miseries, it seems to me strangely lacking in reality. It is shadowy and unsubstantial.   (*The Summing-Up*, 211)

Admittedly Maugham wrote this when past middle age, but the sentiments expressed about life as a dream, so it seems to me, are likely to come up in mid-life, whose dreamlike quality Philip Larkin captures in another way:

> I have started to say
> "A quarter of a century"
> Or "thirty years back"
> About my own life.
> It makes me breathless.
> It's like falling and recovering
> In huge gesturing loops
> Through an empty sky.
>   ("I Have Started to Say", in his *Collected Poems*)

This strange sense of the weight of one's own being and life along with the lightness of what one is and has done is likely first to arise as one enters middle age: that is, I think, how we mark (part of) what it is to be entering this period of life, which is not to say that one cannot experience it at other times – I think that adolescence is such a time, which in certain ways anticipates middle age – or that everyone in middle age experiences it.

Perhaps this uncanny combination of experiences finds something like adequate expression in Hannah Arendt's idea, discussed in *The Human Condition*, that there is a kind of gap or emptiness at the centre of what one is and does. She traces this to the fact that we are each of us inevitably and permanently caught up in a vast web of relations with others, and consequently there is a sense in which our actions fail to achieve what we intend them to achieve. She does not mean, of course, that we cannot sometimes aim at, say, getting some of the things we want and be successful in doing so; of course we can. But she wants nonetheless to stress that very often we simply do not get what we aim for, since others intervene and deflect or modify what we were aiming at, or thought we were aiming at. And even when we get what we aim for the *meaning* of what we get always escapes us, and this is partly because we often do not know what meaning we attach to some deed or set of deeds, but also because the meaning we attach to our deeds is always exposed to reinterpretation, re-evaluation and rejection by others – and by ourselves. But it does not really matter if there are human deeds not subject to such limitations and constraints, because clearly most of them are: certainly the ones that matter to us. All of this delivers an understanding of ourselves and our life, Arendt suggests, in which we feel that there must be an author to one's life, but have no real idea who or what the author is. And this thought is almost unbearable. So we say, according to Arendt, that the real author is God, or the gods, or Nature, or History and so on: all fictions designed to fill in an intolerable spiritual gap. Arendt's teacher Martin Heidegger is sometimes thought of as a philosopher of endings, since he spoke so much about death, while Arendt is seen as a philosopher of beginnings, or natality, on account of her interest in the ways human beings initiate deeds in the world. But in her emphasis on the absence of an author for the life of each of us she is also a philosopher of middle age, since only in middle age, I think, will one start to have a living sense of what she is talking about.

Perhaps Joseph Conrad was getting at the same thing when he remarked in a letter to Edward Garnett that "one's own personality is only a ridiculous and aimless masquerade of something hopelessly unknown" (*Letters from Conrad*, 23). But he also can reasonably be read to mean something else. I have in mind Nietzsche's suggestion in the following passage from *Daybreak*:

> Language and the prejudices upon which language is built are a manifold hindrance to us when we want to fathom inner processes and drives: because, for example, words really only exist for the *superlative* degrees of those processes and drives; and where we lack words, we are accustomed to abandon exact observation because exact thinking there becomes painful ... Anger, hatred, love, pity, desire, knowledge, joy, pain – these are all names for *extreme* states: the milder, middle degrees, not to mention the lower degrees which are continually in play, elude us, and yet it is they which weave the web of our character and destiny ... *We are none of us* that which we appear to be in accordance with the states for which alone we have consciousness and words ... [W]e ... *misunderstand* ourselves ... misread ourselves ...
>
> (*Morgenröte*, §115)

Someone who looks at things this way is likely to feel that the inadequacies of language are not just those connected with understanding the inner life. They are likely to reach further, to a sense that somehow the world itself is too slippery for words to be able to stick to it. Hugo von Hofmannsthal described such a sense in his *Letter of Lord Chandos*, a fictitious letter to Francis Bacon, actually written in 1902 but dated 22 August 1603:

> In short, my case is this: I have completely lost the ability to think or say anything coherently ... At first I gradually found

it impossible to discuss a loftier or more general subject and to use those words that everyone habitually uses without hesitation. I experienced an inexplicable discomfort even uttering the words "mind", "spirit" or "body" ... Gradually, however, these attacks of anguish spread like a corrosive rust. I found the judgements of familiar and everyday conversations, which are offered casually and with thoughtless confidence, so questionable that I had to give up having anything to do with such conversations ... I was filled with an inexplicable anger, which I could only just conceal, whenever I heard such things as: Sheriff N is a bad man, Parson T is a good man; tenant M is to be pitied because his sons are wasters; someone else is enviable because his daughters are thrifty; this family is making its way in the world, that one is going to the dogs. All of that seemed to me as indemonstrable, as mendacious, as empty as one could imagine. I felt myself compelled to look extraordinarily close up at all things that cropped up in such a conversation: just as I once looked at a piece of skin from my little finger under a magnifying glass and it looked like a field full of furrows and holes, so I looked at people and what they did. I could no longer look at them with the simplifying glance of habit. Everything disintegrated into pieces, and the pieces themselves into pieces, and I could understand nothing with one thought. The individual words lapped around me; they congealed into eyes that stared at me and into which I myself had to stare; they are whirlpools which, incessantly turning, make me feel dizzy and lead me into the void.

(*Brief des Lord Chandos an Francis Bacon*)

I do not know how common such an understanding is, or whether it is something that is connected in some particular way with middle age. But I find for myself that one aspect of my experience of middle age is well captured by Hofmannsthal. Such a feeling of the inadequacies of language was, indeed, part of the loss or eclipse of the world that middle age meant for me and which I have been discussing. It might be said that this is all very well, but I too am using such words here, and so was Hofmannsthal; indeed, the latter writes brilliantly about the impossibility of expressing himself or anything else much. This response, while understandable, is, I think, not really to the point. Eliot expressed the reply best:

So here I am, in the middle way, having had twenty years –
Twenty years largely wasted, the years of *l'entre deux guerres* –
Trying to learn to use words, and every attempt
Is a wholly new start, and a different kind of failure
Because one has only learnt to get the better of words
For the thing one no longer has to say, or the way in which
One is no longer disposed to say it. And so each venture
Is a new beginning, a raid on the inarticulate
With shabby equipment always deteriorating
In the general mess of imprecision of feeling,
Undisciplined squads of emotion.

("East Coker", V, in *Collected Poems*)

In a marvellous short portrait of Conrad, Bertrand Russell said of him, "I felt ... that he thought of civilized and morally tolerable human life as a dangerous walk on a thin crust of barely cooled lava which at any moment might break and let the unwary sink into fiery depths" (*Portraits from Memory*, 82). That captures pretty well a central element of the kinds of experiences I have been discussing and of which one might have a keener sense in middle age. Because he saw life in such terms, Conrad emphasized the place and importance of *work* in life. There was, he believed, a particular kind of dignity in the sober exercise of one's duty in the service of one's work, precisely because life is such a perilous affair. Conrad had spent the first part of his life as a merchant seaman, and the kind of work he had in mind was largely active, physical work. In some respects he resembled Wittgenstein, who felt that there was something profoundly unhealthy about life as an academic philosopher and who himself gave up philosophy at various points in his life to work as a gardener. There was for Wittgenstein something *honest* about the kind of labour characteristic of work in a garden. This honesty derived from the sense that the external rhythm of nature, to which the gardener has to be responsive, helps to provide a kind of order to the inner world of the mind. It was also a matter of the fact that gardening provides a focus for the mind's energy, helping it to avoid consuming itself in its own anxious self-questionings.

Perhaps, to return to that, the feeling of death had, or has, for me, a special significance. I said earlier that the sense of contingency in one's identity is stripped from one by the love of one's parents. It is, I think, not surprising therefore that one aspect of the question concerning the contingency of my being who I was astonished to find I am – that I happen to be H's son – was deeply corporeal. I felt in a way ejected from any love that H might have for me, since I could not possibly think of his loving me, and was not – am not – sure I wanted him to. There is, I have suggested, something redemptive in a parent's love for his or her child: the parent loves the child in or through his body, loves him as a body, and this love does not depend on anything such as features of the personality. It is, perhaps, our primary sense of being unconditionally accepted for what we are, and, as such, it provides an image of, or hope for, physical security in the world. I have long felt a sense of the physical or material hostility of the world, and, when I was told about H, I think this sense received a kind of deep and perhaps ineradicable confirmation. It was as if my body, and therefore I, had no possibility of being at home in the world, as if this possibility were decisively and finally placed beyond me. But that is surely an image of death.

***

One thing that all this gave rise to in me was an acute sense of lone-liness. Such loneliness is, I think, characteristic of the experience of mid-life, for that is the time when one is likely to become newly aware of just how hostile the world can be. One sees that good-ness and kindness are rarely rewarded and are often punished; that mediocrity and thoughtlessness are often more successful than genuine insight and imagination; that wealth and other material goods are usually extraordinarily unjustly distributed; that arro-gance and conceit are often the requirements for success and pres-tige; and that goodness is usually largely held in place not by genuine virtue but by fear and anxiety. As Ecclesiastes has it: "I returned, and saw under the sun, that the race is not to the swift, nor the battle to the strong, neither yet bread to the wise, nor yet riches to men of understanding, nor yet favour to men of skill; but time and chance happeneth to them all" (9:11). And to put the point summarily: either you fit in with this, at least much of the time or in many ways, or you go under. Of course, if you are lucky, there will be others around who can help, but, even so I think there is a kind of loneliness here simply in grasping how horribly compromised the world is.

Once again, Bachmann expresses the thought here extraordi-narily well:

When did it all begin? The suppression and thoughtlessness had taken root in him thanks both to friends and enemies shortly after he let himself get embroiled in the squabbles of social life. So it seemed to him. Had he not since then, in his cowardice, led a double life, a many-sided life, simply in order to live at all? Was he not deceiving everyone and himself in countless ways? ... [H]e had discovered that the people around you hurt you, that you yourself hurt them and that there are moments in which one is offended so deeply that all is ash in the mouth – that everyone is offended by others

21

to the point of death. And that all are frightened of death in which alone they can save themselves from the monstrous offence that life is.　　　　　　　　("Das dreißigste Jahr", 23–4)

The word I have translated as "offence" is in the German "*Kränkung*", and its full meaning cannot be captured in English: it carries with it an association to the word "*krank*", meaning "ill" or "sick", and thus Bachmann is saying that life itself is a kind of offensive illness on account of its appalling compromises.

One especially important aspect of this is without doubt the stark discrepancy between people's words and deeds. Everywhere one looks one sees that we all speak much better than we are, partly because we would like to persuade others – and ourselves – that we are not really as bad as we are. Sometimes one can be so disgusted by all this that the only hope seems to lie in silence, but this, of course, is hopeless in the long run if one wants to live anything like a full life outside a monastery. Machiavelli remarked that:

this may be said of men generally: that they are ungrateful, fickle, feigners and dissemblers, avoiders of danger, eager for gain. While you benefit them they are all devoted to you: they would shed their blood for you; they offer you their possessions, their lives, and their sons ... when the need to do so is far off. But when you are hard pressed they turn away.

　　　　　　　　　　　　　　　　　　　　(*The Prince*, 59)

Machiavelli was making a political point, but it clearly has more general application. I think that he is basically right, which does not mean, I hope, that I cannot see goodness where it is. Indeed, accepting such a view can make one rather more generous or tolerant towards others, not because one thinks little of them, but because one expects little of them: a crucial difference in my view. But it is, of course, more or less impossible to see oneself steadily or clearly in such terms, even when one knows it is true and gets intimations of it: the force of self-preservation asserts itself against that insight. And part of this is that one condemns others for things one does oneself, and hardly notices that one is doing so. This is not to say, of course, that none are better than others. But it is to say, I think, that there is a deep truth in Christ's claim that we should not judge others, even if this must inevitably remain an ideal forever beyond the human condition.

Among other things, what is going on in all this is that a person's understanding of morality and moral notions undergoes important changes as he or she gets older. Philosophers have generally not been very interested in exploring this kind of development, and hence there is next to no philosophical literature on middle age. The reasons for this lie deep in the subject, but the main one is that philosophy normally takes itself to be fundamentally and essentially interested in purely conceptual matters, which it conceives of as being quite separate from matters of history: the history of an individual or of a culture. But middle age is a deeply *historical* phenomenon and so philosophy tends to lose it from sight.

But in another way, the problem philosophy has here goes deeper. Walter Jackson Bate indicates what it is in a discussion of Samuel Johnson's entry into middle age:

It is a commonplace of psychology that few people care to dwell consciously on the problems of middle age. To those in their twenties and early thirties, the problems are not yet real. Those already entered on middle age would prefer not to have their attention riveted to it directly lest, like the head of Medusa, it rob them of their stamina and leave them paralyzed. Their first concern is to keep their own balance on what has begun to seem a sort of tightrope, and not look down but rather across – to an end, aim, or purpose. Nor, afterward, is there much interest in dwelling on the traumas of middle age, for the simple reason that few people are confident they are safely past them.   (*Samuel Johnson*, 233–4)

I think it would be fair to say that, in one way therefore, there is no language of middle age. At any rate, there is no such language as there is a language of youth or even old age. Middle age is a kind of psychological and conceptual blank, by which I mean not that there is not much said on it, but that what is said on it is said in the face of the natural tendency of middle age to resist articulation and clarification: it does not naturally offer itself for our investigation.

To return to this: my sense of the compromised nature of life in general terms, itself already very active in my mind from a pretty young age, was heavily focused on, or channelled through, what I saw – and see – as the compromised nature of my mother's relationship with H. An affair between two people each married to another is of its nature compromised anyway – it is a concession to imperatives of thought and feeling that married life is itself intended to repudiate, or anyway to contain, at least as I understand marriage – but there was also something disgusting for me in being the product of an affair involving secret and furtive assignations.

My sense of loneliness was increased, I think, by a particular reaction in me to the compromised sense of the world, which reaction was itself an attempt to overcome that very feeling about life. I was, that is, gripped strongly by an acute desire for purity in my inner life, something that, had I been able to achieve it, would have reduced the sense of the compromised nature of the human scene but which, because I could not achieve it – and I do not think anyone can – only made the compromises seem more aggressive and thus increased my sense of loneliness. This desire in me for purity was a kind of rage, a rage primarily against myself. I felt with renewed force something that had been troubling me increasingly over the years; namely, that I really had no love in me at all since anything that I could offer to anyone like this could not really be love, since it was too deeply bound up with, and held in place by, my own needs and desires – that is, by my own selfishness. I experienced a growing deadness in me, and I came gradually to feel the truth in the idea – an old idea, but, like most such ideas, one that you have to learn for yourself – that to be unable to love another is to be condemned to a kind of ultimate loneliness.

I am not at all sure, really, whether this longing for purity – which is certainly characteristic of religious thought in its best and worse forms – is a common way in which people in middle age experience the compromises of life, although, judging by the character Ryumin in Maxim Gorky's *Summerfolk*, I am not alone:

> [I]f you stare life straight in the face, what do you see? Some inscrutable beast which devours us, and sucks our blood, and mashes our brains just for pleasure! What the devil is it for? And the older you get, the more you become aware of the filth, the banality, the mediocrity, the injustice that surrounds us ... and the more you crave purity and light ...
>
> (*Summerfolk*, 24–5)

Be that as it may, it is without doubt very common for the middle-aged to feel that the life they have set up for themselves – these days, usually, something like marriage, children and a career – has suddenly gone dead on them because it is shot through with compromises and consequences that they simply could not foresee. Bate puts this point extraordinarily well in his discussion of Johnson:

> What is especially involved in the inner life ... is the recognition that begins to deepen in middle age that our "choices" in life, in careers, in marriage, in everything else, are now – with our lives at least half over – bringing completely unexpected and unwelcome chickens home to roost. Or, to change the metaphor, because we selected one fork in the road rather

than another – and did we really "choose" it? – we have not merely forfeited the chance of taking that other fork ... [M]ore distressingly, we find that our "choice" of each fork of the road has brought with it so much that we had never bargained for – so much that we have never wished for, or even dreamed of as an inevitable by-product, in that original idealism or hope that had inspired or hovered about the choices we had made. (*Samuel Johnson*, 235)

One aspect of the experience to which Bate is drawing attention is the sense typical in middle age of being *trapped* in the life one is living. Central here is undoubtedly one's work. When I was a teenager I had a friend whose father was going through what I now see to have been the typical middle age feeling of being trapped in his life. He had dutifully exercised a dull but secure career for about twenty-five years and was now facing about the same stretch of time in the same work. It is obvious to me now that he longed to escape the narrow, repetitive life that his work was for him, although, despite the fact that I could see he disliked his work, I was at the time too young, of course, to understand the exact nature of his suffering.

Central to the way in which work contributes to the sense of being trapped in mid-life is that almost all modern forms of work are deeply bureaucratic: we live, as Theodor Adorno pointed out, in the "administered society", in which work consists largely in the completion of unimaginative and rote tasks whose aims are principally that of promoting their own continued repetition. The kind of individual encouraged by such a system of work is the unthinking conformist, one of whose main concerns consists in securing and retaining a place in the system itself and for whom most forms of learning must remain, in F. R. Leavis's marvellous words, "amassed externalities" (in Mill 1971: 4). To some extent at least we are all like this, because we have to be if we are to survive in such a world.

And in middle age one is most likely to feel keenly burdened by this precisely because at this point in life one will in all probability have secured a reasonably comfortable position in the structure in question. It may be that the phenomenon of middle age being a time that has its own peculiar difficulties is thus something that only arises – at least for large numbers of people – under given social and economic conditions: the modern age may well be an age that encourages such a phenomenon, which is not to say that it has not existed, or does not exist, outside such conditions.

In fact, as Arendt pointed out in *The Human Condition*, work in the modern world tends to take on the form of labour, an activity that does not build a common cultural world but rather contributes simply to our continued biological maintenance as animals. This is the reverse side of its being so deeply bureaucratized: just as such work exists largely for its own sake, losing sight of any purpose or reason it might have outside itself, so it predominantly exists for the maintenance of the individual as a creature that needs food, shelter and warmth simply to go on existing – that is, without purpose or reason beyond the satisfaction of those needs. Unsurprisingly, much of working life tends to become a kind of exhausting, deadening effort.

In one way, Bate's point that the notion of choice becomes problematic for many in middle age could be expressed by saying that life no longer seems to run in a linear fashion. The archaeology on which many embark at this point of life reveals, rather, that there are buried fragments in the soul that, when brought to light, change the meaning of much of what lies on the surface, just as a piece of pottery unearthed can change a historian's sense of a whole tract of human development. The present is not something at the nearest end of one's development, so to speak, but rather a knot in the fabric that lies spread out before one in all directions. This, at any rate, is how Robert Musil puts it in giving us the meditations of Ulrich in *The Man Without Qualities*:

And what occurred to him then was one of those seemingly out-of-the-way and abstract thoughts that so often in his life took on such immediate significance, namely that the law of this life, for which one longs, overburdened as one is and at the same time dreaming of simplicity, was none other than narrative order! This is the simple order that consists in one's being able to say "When this had happened, then that happened". What puts our mind at rest is the simple sequence, the overwhelming multiplicity of life now represented in, as a mathematician would say, a unidimensional order: the stringing upon one thread of all that has happened in space and time, in short, that notorious "narrative thread" of which it then turns out the thread of life consists. Lucky the person who can say "when", "before" and "after"! ... What they [that is, most people] like is the orderly sequence of facts, because it has the look of necessity, and by means of the impression that their life has a "course" they manage to feel somehow sheltered in the midst of chaos. And now Ulrich observed that he seemed to have lost this elementary narrative element ... and no longer followed a "thread", but rather [saw his life] spread out in an infinitely interwoven surface.

(Der Mann ohne Eigenschaften, 650)

But Ulrich has just as much a need of narrative order as the rest of us, and if in middle age you have the sense that your life has taken on the form of "an infinitely interwoven surface", you will probably also crave the order of a narrative thread as a refuge from the chaos.

It is a cliché, of course, to speak of a mid-life crisis in such a context, but only because so many experience it: the details of any given individual's experience are painful enough to make it impertinent to label them in such terms. Eliot expressed it magnificently:

There is, it seems to us,
At best, only a limited value
In the knowledge derived from experience.
The knowledge imposes a pattern, and falsifies,
For the pattern is new in every moment
And every moment is a new and shocking
Valuation of all we have been. We are only undeceived
Of that which, deceiving, could no longer harm.
In the middle, not only in the middle of the way
But all the way, in a dark wood, in a bramble,
On the edge of a grimpen, where is no secure foothold,
And menaced by monsters, fancy lights,
Risking enchantment.

("East Coker", II, in *Collected Poems*)

Eliot's point, among others, is that what we discover in middle age was there all along and will remain. The problems of middle age are not simply problems "in the middle of the way / But all the way ...". There is a kind of astonished recognition at this stage of life that we have been, as George Eliot put it in *Middlemarch*, "well-wadded in stupidity" and could not see this. But more impressive is the fact that there really is no escape from this condition. This state of moral and spiritual provisionality can be fairly unnerving, since it becomes clear how utterly temporary and groping all our most important judgements must be. Perhaps it is fear of this that leads so many people to think that the sign of a thoughtful mind is that it is well stocked with clear opinions on everything important: a view that I cannot but think of as a fiction and an expression of anxiety about how things really are. Indeed, the truth, as it seems to me, is clearly that if there is any wisdom to be gained from the experience of middle age it lies in accepting that reflection is likely to make everything less straightforward and more intractable. And if you agree about that you will be likely to hold your opinions in a certain manner, perhaps with a kind of sceptical or even comic intent.

Samuel Johnson, who long sought such an attitude towards his own opinions, felt that it was partly, but significantly, nourished by being able to take pleasure in the small things of life; like Wittgenstein, he hoped to find solace in gardening. One issue here is that of giving up many of the great plans one had earlier in life, which one can now see are forms of *naïveté* or vanity that distort and deform one's appreciation of the present moment. Giving up such plans can seem – and is – to some extent a loss, a capitulation to exigencies of life that one cannot have chosen, but it is also a form of release, a recognition that what really matters is the quality of one's inner life, which has in many ways little to do with external or socially sanctioned achievements. Hence it is that one of the valuable aspects of middle age as I experience it is that I am so much less frightened of others and their achievements: underneath an other's imposing façade – when it is imposing – I know to lie a self just as anxious or unsure or confused as my own. So if the façade is what makes someone happy then it is not the façade itself that makes him such but his healthy relation to it, which is a matter of his inner life, not the façade as such.

One chief art in life is, then, I think, the capacity to take pleasure in the small things of life, even as these things cross our path unexpectedly. The same kind of idea crops up at the end of Woody Allen's film *Manhattan*. He draws up a kind of list of the things that make life worth living, including Groucho Marx, the second movement of Mozart's Jupiter Symphony, Louis Armstrong, Swedish films, Marlon Brando, Frank Sinatra, Cézanne and his girlfriend's face. In the section entitled "Why I am so clever" of his extremely odd autobiography, *Ecce Homo*, Nietzsche too draws up such a list, including in his tea, cold water, dry air, a clear sky, the south of France and northern Italy, although he more often says what would *not* be on his list: "German cuisine as such – think of all the problems with that! Soup *before* the meal, the boiled meats, the oily and stodgy vegetables, the degeneration of dessert to a paperweight!" ("Warum ich so klug bin", in *Ecce Homo* §1). In any case, it is certainly true that it is astonishingly easy to forget the small pleasures of life, and yet it is these that can really provide a great deal of what makes life worth living; and I think of middle age as a time when one has a better sense of which things in life provide pleasure in this way, since by then, it is to be hoped, one has a somewhat better insight into one's own character.

My sense of loneliness was – and remains – partly a sense of not properly belonging to either of the families between which I stand and to which I am related. This was something of which I had many times had intimations with respect to my Hamilton siblings: a strange, ineffable, mute sense of being somewhat different from them, some deep temperamental division that could only be described in terms of character traits in a very crude way. Hence it was that my first words on being told about H were: "This explains so much!" Something appalling had become clear to me, and it was as if I had always known it, even as if I had been waiting my whole life for this moment. And one way in which I experienced this was in terms of a powerful sense of disassociation from the person that I am. It was as if there was a person in the world – Christopher Hamilton – who had led a life, doing this or that and so on, and that this person was me, but somehow I felt acutely separated from him, as if I were watching from above something or someone other than myself who was going through the motions of some activities essentially unconnected with me, with the *I* that I am. Many people in middle age have testified to something similar, that is, to the feeling that they are alienated from being that particular person *there*: the philosopher Thomas Nagel, for example, has discussed it in a somewhat similar fashion in his book *The View from Nowhere* (ch. IV), although he does not explicitly link it to middle age. However, Nagel was in his late forties when he wrote his book, so perhaps middle age contributed to his having the thoughts and feelings about himself that he did; he certainly grants that there is an issue here of *feeling* these things for oneself, although since he wants to present the issue as a metaphysical problem available to all regardless of the course their different lives may have taken rather than as a matter of personal experience, as I present it, he fights somewhat shy of his own point about *feeling* the force of the issue. Be that as it may, the problem is that it is as if there is no answer to the question "How can I be this person?", since one cannot bring the *I* clearly into connection with this material entity of flesh and blood that is who one is. Or the question might be: "How did I come to be that person, with those character traits, leading this kind of life?" One can imagine how someone else might have come to be that person living that life and so on, but not how one became that person oneself. The world, so it seems in this mood, is populated by a large but finite number of lives and one might have been leading any one of them – so how come I ended up leading *that* one? Arendt expressed some such point by distinguishing *who* one is from *what* one is: *what* I am is given by the list of my characteristics, deeds and so on, but *who* I am is elusive to this, and can only be known, if at all, by others, not by myself. This involves a kind of vertigo, a sort of emptiness over oneself. It is, indeed, another way of getting at the sense of one's life as a dream that I raised earlier. In my case there was the added factor that in one sense *I really am not Christopher Hamilton*, since I am not related by blood to the man who gave me the surname "Hamilton", and when I was told about H I had the feeling that I really was not the person who had done the things Christopher Hamilton had done. I thought for a while of changing my name, since it seemed almost dishonest to give myself out under my present name, and when I saw this name on the cover of books and other things I have written and published, I felt that I had not written them at all, but someone else had, who had, as it were, simply filled in an empty space where my identity might otherwise be or have been.

One thing this brings out is the importance of one's name. In the tenth book of his autobiography *Poetry and Truth*, Goethe remarked "A man's name is not like a mantle which merely hangs about him, but a perfectly fitting garment, which, like the skin, has grown over him, at which one cannot scrape and pull without injuring the man himself" (*Aus meinem Leben: Dichtung und Wahrheit*). In these terms I could say that I felt that my name was like a false skin that had grown over me and which I wanted to slough off. But underneath would be left no skin at all, and H's surname, which I might have taken, would not fit in the least: it would merely hang about me. And when I discovered that my mother had given me the middle name "Francis" because H's three children by his wife have this middle name, I felt as if my identity were being played with. And I felt this because I have had this name all my life and knew nothing of its significance, like a latent disease or like an indication on the skin, designed to mark me out even though I did not know this.

One's name is very deeply bound up with one's sense of identity, arbitrary as having any particular given name is, a fact that Larkin grasped beautifully in his poem about maiden names, finding it mysterious that a woman can drop her surname and take on that of another person: "Marrying left your maiden name unused. / Its five light sounds no longer mean your face, / Your voice, and all your variants of grace ..." ("Maiden Name", in *Collected Poems*). As Larkin said, in commenting on this poem: "I often wonder how women survive the transition [from one name to another]: if you're called something, you can't be called something else" (*Further Requirements*, 55). Of course, these days women less often take on their husband's name when they marry: perhaps they have more of a sense of who they are than was once the case. And more generally, W. H. Auden comments:

Throughout life our existence is profoundly influenced by names – names of persons we meet and love, names of characters, whether in history or fiction, who embody for us what we mean by goodness, justice, courage, names of artists and scientists who have helped to form our conception of life and the world. Indeed, one might say: "Give me a list of the names in your life, and I will tell you who you are".

(*Secondary Worlds*, 107)

But if, like me, you find that from the list of names in your life your *own* name is missing, then you cannot tell who you are.

In a brilliant passage, into which are compressed many deep experiences of life, Gerard Manley Hopkins wrote:

[W]hen I consider my selfbeing, my consciousness and feeling of myself, that taste of myself, of *I* and *me* above and in all things, which is more distinctive than the taste of ale or alum, more distinctive than the smell of walnut or camphor, and is incommunicable by any means to another man … [I see that] … [n]othing else in nature comes near this unspeakable stress of pitch, distinctiveness, and selving, this selfbeing of my own.   (*Poems and Prose*, 146)

The image of the *taste* of oneself captures, it seems to me, something absolutely right. And, indeed, I would say that one has such a sense for, and of, the people around one. This is because, in my view, friendships and the attraction of sexual desire are, in the end, deeply mysterious because they rest on an ineffable sense of the style or manner of another person. This is brought out lyrically in Adalbert Stifter's short story "Brigitta":

In human life there are often things and relations which are not immediately clear to us and the reason for which we are not readily able to unearth. They usually work secretly, the result of a certain beautiful and gentle attractive force on the soul. In the face of someone who is ugly we find an inner beauty which we are not able there and then to bring into connection with his intrinsic value, whereas the features of another who is generally considered to possess great beauty leave us cold and empty. In just the same way, we sometimes feel drawn to someone whom we actually do not know at all: we like his way of moving, his manner appeals to us, and we are sad when he leaves us and have a certain longing for, even love for, him when we think of him years later.

("Brigitta", 19)

Be that as it may, to realize that your name no longer fits, or has never fitted, as I did, is in part to feel that you have gone through life with a mistaken understanding of your *feeling* for yourself, as if you had been drinking something that turned out to be adulterated.

I think in a way that the sense of loneliness in middle age was, at any rate for me, a feeling of inner emptiness, as if there were a gaping hole in the centre of what I am. This feeling of emptiness was one, I think, that I had been carrying around with me all my life, but had come to the fore in middle age as a result of my experiences. Others, too, have this feeling about themselves in middle age. Perhaps we all do. I think of this emptiness as a need for love and affection. Yet running along with that is an image of independence, of a longing to have no such need. Hence, when I have had the closeness I seek I have sometimes easily felt suffocated and felt a deep desire to escape. Richard Wollheim tells us in his memoir of his childhood that he was often subject to similar feelings. He describes how, as a solider in London at the beginning of the Second World War, he engaged the services of a prostitute. She led him to her room up some stairs. He writes:

> Each time I recall the event, what is brought back to me with painful vividness is an alternation of mood from which I have never learnt to escape altogether ...: a fierce, overbearing loneliness giving way to a suffocating togetherness, the two separated by no more than the shutting or opening of a front door, or the climbing of a staircase, or just the turning of a key in an innocent enough lock. (*Germs*, 238)

I am certain that my inner conflict between a need for closeness, warmth, affection and love, together with a kind of horror in the face of these and a need to escape them, has blighted many of the relationships I have had. Since I am baffled in the face of my needs in this respect, it is hardly surprising that others have been. But at least the struggles in this regard have made clear to me how completely hopeless it is trying to change anyone else: something that a friend of mine, in middle age, called "one of life's great lessons". Just as one has to learn to cope with one's own character, so one has to learn to cope with others' characters. This is not to deny, of course, that one can affect others by being around them a fair bit, but it does mean, first, that it is pointless trying *directly* to change someone else and, secondly, that any effect one has on another is like the effect a gardener might have on a tree: it can grow in this or that direction under his influence, but all the basics of what it is are fixed and something over which he has no control.

That may seem a melancholy reflection, but actually I find it rather consoling, since it is a further source, in addition to that already mentioned, for being more tolerant of others. And in mid-life we are able to be more tolerant with ourselves, too, I think. To some extent at least we all see in middle age the ways in which we are each inadequate, ridiculous or hopeless, but we have also come to learn that, really, nothing here will change. If we are lucky, we are able through this insight to forgive ourselves better, and accept better what we are because there is no possibility of change. What is needed is to try to structure the external details of life so that they nurture and bring out what is good and positive in us. There is here, I think, a kind of a practical, realistic sense of one's strengths and limitations, of what it makes sense to ask of oneself and what it is hopeless to demand of oneself.

***

Running throughout much of what I have said is, of course, the meaning of flesh and blood. What bound and binds me to H is the relation of being of his flesh and blood, and it is this that binds each of us to our parents and to our siblings, if we have any, regardless of, or behind, anything else that may bind us, such as the life we have shared with them.

There is, surely, something at once completely obvious about why it is that we feel bound to others by being of their flesh and blood, even if we have never met them, and also utterly mysterious about it. And one reason for this is at least in part because our sense of being bound to our parents in this way inherits, as it were, its strangeness from sex: from the sexual act that brings us into existence in the first place. That is, to put the point bluntly, we feel bound by flesh and blood to our parents partly because they had sex with one another, and sex is itself something whose power over us is at once clear and obvious, yet also deeply perplexing. One aspect of that power is, indeed, the sheer force or urgency of sexual desire, in which we feel overwhelmed by something that seems both deeply within and yet to overwhelm us from without. That aspect of sexual desire involves or, at any rate, may well involve, a certain aggressive quality. But the power sexual desire has over us also has a different side or aspect. This is the power in the need of tenderness and warmth with, and from, another human being, and in the desire to give these to another. When

such gentleness finds sexual expression we are dealing with a kind
of sexual desire, or an aspect of it, at the furthest end from anything
brutal or crude. And in truth there is something utterly baffling
about the need we all feel for the warmth of physical contact with
another human being. I mean that it is a need beyond choice and
beyond judgement, primordial and primitive. Further, there just
is something similarly baffling about the need, for example, to be
physically close to *this* person, and not anyone else. And such need
carries or expresses a sense of the absolute irreplaceability of the
other. In a way, I think, one's feelings about being bound to one's
parents are feelings about the fact that this kind of regard – this
kind of physical regard – for each other existed between them. I
do not mean, of course, that one needs to entertain in any detail
any thoughts about what went on between them when one was
conceived. I mean, rather, something more like this: to discover
or fear that such tenderness as I have mentioned between them
was not possible, is to feel a kind of sense of a failure of a deep
human possibility, a possibility that is itself a source of consolation
in, and for, our condition. Even if one knows or suspects that one
was conceived in an urgent and coarse sexual act, this need not, as
such, matter much to one, if one also knows that there were other
sexual possibilities for one's parents.

Even if a person were to discover that he is the product of a
rather crude one-night stand and had never really known his
parents, I think that it is partly the nature of human sexuality that
would make it unsurprising for him to go, or wish to go, in search
of them. This may depend in part on a sense of human sexuality
as having, let us say, better possibilities. Be that as it may, there is,
as I have already suggested, something about the peculiar physical
intimacy – the intimacy of the flesh – of sex that is partly responsible for one's sense of being bound to one's parents. This is itself
partly because sex is not, of course, simply about physical intimacy:
only some need or longing of the deepest spiritual kind could drive

two people to lower all the barriers that normally or naturally stand between human beings. Of course, that need not mean these needs or longings must be especially noble or dignified, but they are deeply revelatory of any given individual's sense of himself or herself, however implicit or unarticulated that is. But beyond that, there is something about this act – this act of such physical intimacy, the point, as it were, of complete collapse of physical distance between two people – which matters enormously, whatever else is the case. At any rate, it matters to me that my mother and H had sex, and if I found out that he had impregnated her by some artificial means then I am not at all sure I would feel the same way about him. I am not clear about what I would feel, but I am pretty confident that it would be different. And I am also fairly confident that most other people would have the same feeling in my situation. My sense of being bound to H by flesh and blood is deeply caught up with the acknowledgment that he went to bed with my mother. It is caught up, that is, with the fact that they met in their flesh with one another and meant something to each other as creatures of flesh and blood.

But this way of being bound to H – I mean, by being of his flesh and blood – is replete with many of the meanings these have for human beings. One can put the point this way: to say of myself that I share H's flesh, or am of his blood, is to say something that brings with it multiple resonances. One of these is of the *life* of flesh and blood. To speak of my being of H's flesh and blood is to say immediately, even if only implicitly – although the implicit meaning lies near the surface, so to speak – that I owe him my life, that he has given me life. But saying this kind of thing might in many contexts have no real point, or a different point: say, where there never was any doubt about paternity. In my case, however, it marks out something important; namely, that I owe H my life in a way in which I do not owe K my life, in spite of all that the latter did for me. And if someone were to say that there is, after all, a way in which I owe K my life, since he took me on as his son, then, understood in one way, I would not dispute this. But to insist on it in such a way as to silence the thought that I owe H something that I do not owe K would be to have failed to grasp the significance of H in my life.

But the resonances of the idea of flesh and blood extend further and deeper. One meaning here concerns the extraordinary *vulnerability* of the flesh. It is astonishing how precarious one's existence in the world is, and this lies in the intense vulnerability and, as one might put it, helplessness, of the flesh. This is something that many of us in the West are lucky enough to be able these days largely to ignore or forget, since we live in an age of extraordinary material wealth, plenty and comfort. But the basic point remains, of course, and it comes to the fore when, for example, we are ill or suffer injury. And when we are ill or injured, we are suddenly made aware of how lucky we have been to have been spared these at other times.

The vulnerability of the flesh at this level is something we all share as human beings. But to speak of one's being of the flesh and blood of one's parents is to say something particular about that vulnerability. This might be in a more or less banal way; for example, I have discovered that I could inherit from H a certain genetic weakness of the eyesight and, had I not known about him, I would not have known that I am exposed to this risk. But beyond this there is a sense that what certain philosophers call one's being-in-the-world is deeply bound up with sharing one's parents' flesh and blood. For there are certain contexts in which it makes sense to say, and is worthwhile saying, that one *is* one's body. And this is one of them. In finding out about H, I was made newly aware of the body that I have – that I *am*.

Here is a way at getting at what I mean: to know that one is the product of an adulterous affair, with all that this involves by way of urgent physical and emotional need, betrayal and falsehood, frustration and failure, and moments – I assume – of furtive happiness, casts one's own experience of, or thought about, such things in a particular light. One could say: H was deeply vulnerable to the needs and longings of the body, by which I mean that it makes sense to speak of the needs of his soul, in having the affair, as needs of the body because of the centrality and importance of the body in such a relationship. And I feel in a way that I carry around his vulnerability to his body, his vulnerability *as* his body, in me. By this I mean that I have a deeper and keener sense than I had before of the weakness of human beings in confrontation with their own body.

I suppose there is a way in which I forgive H for doing what he did. It may seem odd that such an idea is relevant at all, since what he did he did before I even existed, and I am quite sure that he did not intend to make my mother pregnant. But the feeling remains. This is because I did not want him as my father: I wanted K to be my father. And I had the fantasy that I could be exactly as I am but be K's son, not H's. It is not, of course, that I am fully satisfied by being who I am: far from it. It is rather that I have, as it were, become rather used to being who I am, and have projected that being into the future and, in a different way, into the past. So I had to forgive H for being my father. And this is one version of something that we all have to face at some point. Larkin of course famously wrote:

> They fuck you up, your mum and dad.
>   They may not mean to, but they do.
> They fill you up with the faults they had
>   And add some extra just for you.
>
> ("This Be The Verse", in *Collected Poems*)

The first line is very well known and its power is somewhat lost on us, especially now we use the expletive all the time. But Larkin is right: it is, one might say, part of being a parent that one gets things wrong – which is of course not to deny that some make a better job of it than others. In any case, one way or another we all have to forgive our parents: for what they are and what they did. It is in middle age that such a need is likely to become especially clear, and it is also then that we might, with a bit of luck, be able to do this, since at that age we become particularly clear that they were, or are, just human, all too human, precisely because we see how we are ourselves just this and no more.

Of course, I ought to forgive my mother as well as H. But, in truth, I have not been able to forgive my mother for much of her treatment of me, and I regard that as a failing on my part, partly because I can attach no substantive content to the thought that she might have behaved differently: it would simply not have been in what she is to have done so. So the best I have been able to do is to have nothing to do with her, which means that at least I do not resent her. H, my father, was one of many lovers she had – probably the first – and she introduced many of them to her children: between her mid-thirties and mid-fifties she was driven by sexual and erotic forces that she could hardly control and did not understand, but she saw in them expressions of love that made her consistently mistake herself and the men to whom she was attracted. That was one of the reasons that she took a kind of perverse pride in being excessively physically demonstrative towards the men in her life in the presence of her children and others, and had a certain contemptuous attitude towards those who could not see these vulgar displays as expressions of a magnificent love which all ought to celebrate. For it was, I am sure, love that she really wanted, and she became adept at persuading herself that she had found it, confusing it again and again with obsessive infatuation. Many of her relationships she discussed with me, treating me as her confidant either as she should not have done at all or when I was far too young; I was probably no more than nine or so when this began. But even as she attacked in this and other ways the idea of my being a child and expressed a resentment against my being so, she was also extremely possessive and did not really want me to grow up into independence, seeking in numerous ways to instil a fear of the world in me as a method of keeping me in her power. And with regard to the men in her life, there was something in her that needed to infantilize them in order to make them dependent on her, and having achieved this she would abandon them with disgust. She manipulated her own emotions, but was, in fact, controlled by them: she was at their mercy even as she exploited them. And her emotional immaturity and her incapacity to question her own feelings and motives were an aspect of her inability to respond to her children's emotional needs as they grew older: she was the kind of mother who was excellent at putting meals on the table, but utterly hopeless at understanding complex demands of the inner life. When I found myself at the age of sixteen in a state of turmoil and despair, she disowned me, and some time later allowed her then lover, who was living with us, to throw me out of the house because of a disagreement I had with him. She also despised K and taught me to do the same, partly by using me, when I was still a child, as a go-between in their mutually destructive relationship. I still feel ashamed for my attitude towards K at that time, although I know I was a child and unable to judge correctly what was going on. Through all this there ran in my mother a kind of self-righteousness, a moralizing, that she was often clever enough to get others to mistake for integrity. Indeed, I think that one of the deepest needs of her life has been the preservation of a sense of her own moral probity, and there is a way in which, for her, thinking has always made it so. In a sense, she has always seen herself as one of the elect, predestined for moral salvation regardless of the details of her behaviour and thought. There were, of course, good things in my relationship with her, but in retrospect – and this was even vaguely so at the time – these things seem to me tainted by an atmosphere of a kind of humourless and morbid sexual intrigue that she more or less permanently created around herself. When I found out about H the last possibility of my having anything like a healthy relationship with her was shattered, not least because she took it that I ought to be glad that she had deliberately conceived me when her affair with H was exposed: "I couldn't have H, so I wanted something from him", was the way she explained her motivation. She could not understand that this is something I can see only as a further sign of her reckless self-absorption, not of genuine love for me, as she understands it.

Wollheim said that he reached a point in life when he wanted to change his mother: not change what his mother was like, but "change her for someone else" (*Germs*, 175). Perhaps it is in middle age that this fantasy is most likely to strike. At any rate, just as I have wished, incoherently, to be as I am but have K and not H as my father, so too I have wished, like Wollheim, that my mother be someone else. Indeed, I think that finding out about H made this thought alive for me, since I could not help but speculate what it would have meant for me to have discovered that I had been mistaken, or misled, as to the identity of my mother, not my father. But the difference, of course, is that my thoughts about H have nothing to do with his character, whereas those about my mother concern nothing but her character. In middle age, when our own personality becomes much clearer, it is typical, I think, to see our parents in us, and, although we may well be grateful for much that they have given us, I am sure that the feeling I have about H and my mother – that I do not wish them to be in me – although perhaps somewhat unusual in its urgency or pointedness for me, is in another way quite typical for this period of life: it is part of seeking to become reconciled with who we are.

Raimond Gaita has said that the expression "of my own flesh and blood" is an expression in the language of love, and not an expression of some pre-theoretical kind awaiting elucidation in, say, the language of biology (*The Philosopher's Dog*, 193). I am sure he is right that it is not an expression that needs such scientific clarification, but it might just as easily be an expression in the language of disgust as of love. I imagine that many of the Christian saints have seen it in that way. Certainly the Christian thinker Søren Kierkegaard did: "[T]he entrance to this room [life] is a nasty, muddy, humble stairway and it is impossible to pass without getting oneself disgustingly soiled, and admission is paid by prostituting oneself" (*Journals and Papers: Vol I*, 339). In any case, where love might be expected, or hoped for, resentment can easily grow and I must admit that, in speaking of my being of H's flesh and blood, and in thinking of what this might mean in terms of love, I feel a certain resentment at my inability to love him and my sense that I ought to. That is part of what I mean, of course, by saying that I have to forgive H, forgive him for being my father: I cannot love him because I cannot really *feel* him to be my father, although I experience a demand – from myself – that I do so, partly because I am, indeed, of his flesh and blood. It is as if thinking of myself as being of his flesh and blood invites me into a relationship of love with him, yet, because of the peculiar course my life has taken, the same idea repels and excludes me and I am judged as failing in something demanded of me. I am sure that many people think of their parents in the same way, even as they have had, let us say, a more straightforward relationship with them than I have had with mine; although, of course, part of what I am saying is that no one's relationship with his or her parents is straightforward.

Perhaps part of what I am getting at is a sense that, when I was told about H, I felt myself instantly to be illegitimate: a bastard. The thought was, as I say, instant; it came to me the moment I was told. These days, when sexual morality is loosening greatly – for some, almost to the point of collapse – no one seems much to feel the weight of the word *bastard*. But for me it is now profoundly loaded with pain. And I thought of Edmund in Shakespeare's *King Lear*, the bastard son of Gloucester, bitter, angry and with a sense of being excluded. I knew – I know – the rage at being a bastard, although in my case my rage was, or is, much more directed towards myself than anyone else. But I now envy my Hamilton siblings in the kind of way that Edmund envies his half-brother Edgar, Gloucester's legitimate son. I envy them for being full-blooded Hamiltons, for their being, as it were, of a clean or uncompromised strain of blood, and because I am, looked at from the present point of view, a kind of mongrel. There is a sense of shame in this, and for a long time after I found out about H I could speak of it only to those closest to me: I felt ashamed at what I had discovered and ashamed at my being what, and who, I am.

The flesh is the face. When Wittgenstein said, as I noted earlier, that the human body is the best picture of the human soul, I sometimes think he should have said: the human face is the best picture of the human soul. And when George Orwell remarked that by forty everyone has the face he deserves, he was making an important observation on middle age; namely, that at forty, or around then – the point is not one that appeals to the literal-minded – one sees in one's own face what one has to live with, what one has become and what one might hope for in the future. The art of portraiture is, in part, the art of exploring exactly that. And if there is *one* artist who is supreme in this, then this is Rembrandt.

Indeed, Rembrandt is not only *the* artist to explore his own face, he is also – at any rate, this is plausibly suggested by a haunting essay written on him by Jean Genet, who in fact wrote two essays on the painter – the artist of the *body*. At one point in one of the essays – it carries the bizarre title "What Remains of a Rembrandt Torn Up Into Neat Little Squares and Chucked Down the Bog" – Genet writes:

> [W]hen I see only the bust or head of people (Hendrijke in Berlin), I can't help imagining them standing in manure. The chests breathe. The hands are warm. Bony, knotted, but warm. The table of the Cloth Makers' Guild is resting on straw, the five syndics smell of manure and dung. Under Hendrijke's

skirts, under the fur-lined cloaks, under the frock coats, under the painter's extravagant robe, the bodies dutifully carry out their functions: they digest, they are hot, they are heavy, they smell, they shit. – However delicate her face is and serious her gaze, *The Jewish Bride* has an arse. You can smell it. Any instant now she can raise her skirts. She can sit down, she's got what it takes. ("Ce qui est resté d'un Rembrandt ...", 21–2)

But Genet also suggests, in his other essay on Rembrandt, "Rembrandt's Secret", that Rembrandt's art shows a progression throughout his life towards a kind of purity that is the destruction of the flesh or, perhaps better, its nothingness.

Towards the end of his life, Rembrandt became good. Whether it retracts it, breaks it, or masks it, maliciousness makes a screen between the world. Maliciousness, and every form of aggression, and everything we call character traits, our humours, our desires, eroticism, and vanities. Pierce the screen, then, to see the world approach! But Rembrandt did not seek out this goodness – or detachment, if you like – to observe a moral or religious rule ... or to earn a few virtues. When he commits what we call his characteristics to the fire, it is in order to have a purer vision of the world, and with it to make a truer work of art. I think at bottom he didn't care about being good or mean, angry or patient, rapacious or generous ... He had to be nothing more than a gaze and a hand. Moreover, by this egoistic path, he had to win ... that kind of purity, so evident in his last portraits that we are almost hurt by it. But it is by the narrow path of painting that he arrives there. ("Rembrandt's Secret", 88–9)

What this suggests is that Rembrandt is for Genet, and for anyone who shares Genet's view of him, the painter of middle age.

And this is because Rembrandt understands the immense *weight* of the flesh and its complete *lightness*, an understanding that reflects and supports the sense in middle age of one's life itself as immensely heavy and yet extraordinarily light, in the kind of way I discussed earlier. To be of flesh and blood in middle age is to be simultaneously profoundly *here* in the world, and yet to be beyond it. In that sense, it is to be caught up – or, rather, knowingly caught up, for we are always in this condition, whether we know it or not, but in middle age we know it – in the way in which the world empties itself of itself, as W. G. Sebald so strikingly put the thought in his novel *Austerlitz*. The world's material being is diminished or exhausted as creatures die and things are destroyed; and one's own body, felt in middle age to be so heavily present as part of that material, is experienced as caught up in that diminution or exhaustion. I remember when George Harrison, the former Beatles lead guitarist, died in 2001. A colleague of mine at the time, who was old enough to consider himself at the tail end of Harrison's generation, said to me that he felt as if "the first one had fallen over the edge". He meant, I think, that he saw himself as caught up in Harrison's death, aware that the world was beginning to empty itself of that generation of which he was a member. And Ian MacDonald wrote in the preface to the second edition of his fascinating book on the Beatles: "When Harrison died, a shiver must have passed through a generation which thereby felt its mortality suddenly a bit more acutely" (*Revolution in the Head*, xiii). Of course, many rock musicians from Harrison's generation had already died, but they usually died in "extreme" circumstances: Harrison's death sent that shiver down the spine of his generation in a way that, say, Keith Moon's or John Lennon's did not, because the former died of a drug overdose and the latter was murdered. These thoughts my former colleague and MacDonald had about Harrison were no doubt helped by Harrison's immense importance for his and later generations, but I do not think they depended on that; they just depended on a sense of connection with him – a sense of material connection, as well as fellowship with another thinking, reflecting person.

The purity at which Rembrandt aimed and which we see in the last portraits is surely the purity that comes from Rembrandt's being able to invest his own face – and therefore his own life – with an eternal significance precisely through an intense exploration of its transient, fleeting phases. It is often the case that we can have such a sense of eternity precisely through the transient or passing. For example, the eponymous character in Sebald's novel *Austerlitz* describes evenings on which he would go as a boy with his uncle to attract and watch moths in the night. Sebald writes:

> All the shapes and colours merged in a pearl-grey haze; there were no contrasts, there was nothing to differentiate. There were only flowing mixtures, pulsating with light, an unbroken blur from which only the most fleeting appearance emerged, and oddly enough – I can remember this exactly – it was precisely the fleetingness of these appearance that gave me at that time something like a feeling for eternity.
>
> (*Austerlitz*, 143)

Middle age, just because it lies at the mid-point of life, is, I think, the point in life that most invites comprehension as a strange combination of the transient and eternal, the fleeting and the permanent. And if we *see* this anywhere it will be in the flesh and blood – in the body and the face: in the body which is both a peak and the beginning of collapse, and in a face that one has deserved. But perhaps only a great artist like Rembrandt can enable one to *see* the truth in this.

***

Middle age is the quintessential period in life to suffer from nostalgia, a seductive but unhealthy emotion. It is very common at this time of life to regret the loss of the past. In my case, I had spent all my adult life seriously trying to leave the past behind, largely because, as a result of various experiences I had in my teens, I had been left depressed and lost for many years, and I was taken over by a sense that I needed to make up for a huge amount of wasted time. I invested a vast quantity of energy in my work, and was like a man hunted down, or haunted, by the past, always seeking to be one step ahead. I studied ferociously, but found myself beginning to be exhausted at about the time my brother told me about H. My past suddenly caught up with me and overwhelmed me. This experience of the past may have been more sudden than with others in middle age, for whom things may develop more slowly, but it is typical of the sense of things many people have at this time of life.

Music was very important in this experience, and I listened again to some music that I had last heard when I was young, in my early teens. Most of it was rubbish, but it carried for me a kind of nostalgic charm because it was, and is, so deeply bound up with certain formative influences in my life. Similarly, I re-read some of the books I had read as a teenager. And the reason why in middle age such things from the past suddenly re-emerge in, and into, one's consciousness, is that they carry with themselves a more or less private system of signs: they are linked with the events of one's life at that time, with the clothes one wore, the friends one had, the cafes one went to and so on. In returning to them, one returns not so much to their obvious qualities – aesthetic qualities, as this might be – but to their qualities in relation to one's world as it then was.

It is well known, of course, that such things as music have in this way great nostalgic potential. They can carry very strongly an acute sense of loss. In a way, of course, this is – from the perspective of mid-life – the loss of youth and past, the sense of the world as an intoxicating arena of possibility, hope, potential and experiment. But it is more than that. This is because one of the oddities of nostalgia is that it is possible to be nostalgic for a past that was, in fact, deeply painful. A good example of this is provided by Joseph Mitchell in his marvellous account of Joe Gould's life, *Joe Gould's Secret*. Gould has been talking of his boyhood home in Norwood close to which there were tanneries that exuded a distinctive smell, "a musky, vinegary, railroady smell". Years later, indeed in middle age, while living the life of a bohemian, mainly around Greenwich Village, Gould says:

> Even today, I sometimes get really quite painfully homesick for Norwood. A sour smell that reminds me of the tanneries will bring it on, such as the smell from a basement down in the Italian part of the Village where some old Italian is making wine. That's one of the damnedest things I ever found out about human emotions and how treacherous they are – the fact that you can hate a place with all your heart and soul and still be homesick for it. (*Joe Gould's Secret*, 70)

It is unclear why even a past that was painful can become the object of nostalgic longings. It may be that, once pain and suffering are over, it is impossible properly to occupy again the feelings one then had, and so the past loses (some of) its awfulness. It may be, more darkly, that there is something in pain and suffering that flatters us. This has been suggested by George Steiner:

> [W]hy does human sensibility, in its creative and analytic motions, find the tragic to be more elevated, more fascinating, more conducive to major aesthetic forms and metaphysical suggestion, than it does the comic? Is there something in "tragedy" which not only seduces imagination and intellect but *flatters* them, as "comedy" does not? ... Even where it is deeply personal, acute, and scarring (there perhaps most) – why is it that something in us feels good when we report disaster? Why is it that, deep within us, even the sickness of a

child or the death of one close to us flatters, where the comic does not? The comic does not flatter sensibility. It does not bribe consciousness. We recount tragic experiences in which we have been involved, to which we have been witness, with an altogether different intonation of *dignitas* and pathos than we do their comic counterparts.

("Tragedy, Pure and Simple", 534)

This is an unsettling thought, of course. Perhaps my very writing of this book testifies to the fact that there is some truth in it. I hope it is false, but I suspect it is true, at least some of the time or in some contexts. In any case, it may be that even if what Steiner says is true and this delivers one reason why we can be nostalgic for a painful past, another reason for this could be that our own individual past is so deeply what we are: in a way, it is – or seems to be – the one thing that cannot be taken away from us, something that absolutely cannot be held in common, even when we have shared the past with others.

But beyond all this, the past can become an intense object of longing for other reasons. What I have in mind is that it seems very deeply rooted in many people – one might even say, in human nature – to have an understanding of the past, a fantasy of the past, in which all was well, or at any rate a great deal better than it is now. But at the same time there is in many people a sense that some time or other, somewhere or other in the past, they made some terrible mistake or committed some terrible error, but they do not know what it was, yet it is a mistake with which they have to live for the rest of their lives. That the past can have such a character for many people is one reason why it can be such an object of longing. And perhaps these two sides of one's sense of the past find expression in such stories as that of Adam and Eve's eating of the Tree of Knowledge of Good and Evil: a halcyon past wrecked by some absurd deed.

We are dealing here with the extraordinarily murky territory of human memory. And it is so murky because, far from its being the case that human memory is a reliable recorder of past events, it is more like a kind of mechanism for the generation of fantasies that latch on to events from the past, not merely colouring them in the process, but changing them. Even when one sincerely and honestly tries to recall one's past – and even where this is done under favourable and non-stressed conditions – one is faced by memory's extraordinary unreliability, slipperiness and elusiveness. Memory is the telling of stories, and all storytelling is construction and invention: this is selected rather than that; this thought is placed next to that feeling and not some other to highlight it; that vague impression is hardened into a "memory" by speaking of it in a certain way; and so on. And beyond that, we are faced with all kinds of self-deception, retellings of the past in our own interests or to make us look more decent or honourable than is in fact the case, and forms of self-justification and special pleading. Hence it is that I am inclined to think that the nostalgia one has in middle age for one's childhood and youth is very largely nourished by fantasies of various kinds. But this, of course, does not make the phenomenon less real or less painful: perhaps quite the opposite.

There is another aspect to the treacherous nature of memory; namely, that concerning how much one actually *wants* to remember, which itself is linked closely with the question of how much one can *bear* to remember. Middle age is the time of life in which one sees how important it is to be able to forget a great deal in order to live healthily. We have a tendency to assume that it is always good to remember. But this is not so: we need to be able to forget because otherwise we are faced with the constant presence of the ways in which our own life has been a force for ill in others' lives, which seems to me, at any rate, to be much harder to bear than is the way in which others' lives have been a force for ill in our own. One reason why we think it good to remember is because we suppose that this provides us with a kind of control and freedom: if I remember, so the thought goes, then I know better what and who I am, and I am better able to get control over that and thus free myself from it. Of course, there is some truth in that, but at the same time it is, I think, in some ways naively optimistic: why should it not be the case that knowing better who and what I am will lead to despair? And if I remember the awful things I have done to others, why does this make me less likely to do them again to others? After all, if I reflect on the ways I have hurt others and take myself to have understood what and why I did what I did, then it might be that this makes me more likely to do them again because my increasingly refined sense of what I have done makes my self-deceptions all the more intractable and elusive to perception. I treat another badly, let us say, and then reflect on my behaviour in a way that is so subtle that I am more likely to do the same thing again to someone else because my refined sensibility about what I am doing fools me into thinking I am actually doing something else. The point is not that one should not remember, but that one needs to know when to remember and when to forget; one needs a balance, which will always be precarious, between the two.

In my own case, of course, one of the things I cannot forget is that I am H's son. I have often been asked whether I am glad I know. Would I not have preferred to remain in ignorance? The question cannot be answered: it would require me to be able to remember what it was like not to know yet all the while knowing, since only in this way could I get some sense of a comparison in nature between being in ignorance and not being so. That is, I no longer remember what it was like not to know, so I cannot say whether I preferred that state. And I cannot now imagine what it would be like to be as I am but not knowing, for I am as I am now with this knowledge. These problems are not a matter of a lack of imagination on my part; they are, rather, part of the very nature of human memory, which itself limits the imagination by making certain ways of understanding one's identity impossible – and others inevitable. But my very writing of this book is itself caught up in the toils of memory, since I am remembering all these things in order to forget them: I write of them so that I can erase them from my memory. But if I were to forget them, I would no longer be who I am. My remembering is intended to be the act of forgetting; it is not just that the former is a means to the latter. They are intended to be one and the same: perfect self-coincidence coinciding with perfect self-displacement. Does this mean that I want to cease to be who I am? What I want is to be exactly who I am, but free of being just that. Middle age is, one might say, the key moment of this fantasy in life.

None of these thoughts about the treacherous nature of memory is meant to deny the reality of loss in middle age *vis-à-vis* one's youth. But it is to say that it is hopeless to attempt to become completely clear about just what one's youth was and therefore what, exactly, it is that one has lost. In a way, one could say that what one has lost is a kind of *mood*: precisely the mood of youth. And that mood is itself, I think, diffuse and vague. If one asks what it is that one longs for, what it is that is the focus of one's nostalgia and sense of loss, then it is nothing other than one's youth as a whole as a kind of undifferentiated, non-specific *presence*. Of course, we may fix on this or that as moments of happiness or freedom, and we may say that this is what we regret the loss of. And while that is no doubt true, there is also a kind of generalized sense that it is not so much this or that which is regretted as what they intimate about the mood of one's life at that time. This is, I think, why many of those who experience in middle age the sense of loss of which I am now speaking feel that they simply cannot say *what* it is that they have lost. In a sense, we are dealing in one way with something like the feeling one can have on being moved by a passage of music or poetry: all attempts to say just what it is about the music or poetry that moves one founder, and one is left simply gesturing at the work. This does not mean one can say nothing in elucidation, but it does mean that what one says is condemned to being largely inadequate to get at one's sense of what it is that moves one here.

The mood, if one tries to describe it, remains, I have suggested, vague. One might say that it is the mood before life has had a chance to wear one down or take its toll on one: before, for example, one has grasped how full of compromises life is, to put it in terms I used earlier. But because, as I have said, one cannot be more precise than this, this is one reason, I think, why one is likely in middle age to feel that language has itself become increasingly elusive to one: that it has given out on one, or given one up. This is not just the sense that one does not have words to articulate some of one's deepest inner states, feelings, moods and so on. It is also, as I said earlier, as if language can no longer get a grip on the world, as if the world has become slippery or impervious to language.

Yet perhaps the vagueness of this mood is somewhat attenuated after all by some thoughts offered by Jean Améry in the course of an investigation of ageing. He writes:

> [The] future into which the young tumble ... is ... not time at all: it is *world* or, more exactly, it is *space*. The young say of themselves that they have time before them. But what really lies before them is the world, which they absorb and by which they let themselves at the same time be branded. The idea is that the old have life behind them, but this life that is no longer actually lived is nothing but time gathered up, lived, passed away. The less time we think we have before us ... the more time there is *in* us ... Characteristically, one is more likely to say of a young person that the *world* is open to him rather than that he has time before him .... To be old or even just to feel oneself ageing means to have time in one's body and in what we call ... one's soul. To be young is to throw one's body into a time that is *no time at all*, but life, world, and space. (*On Ageing*, 14–15)

For the old, the present and the future are engulfed by the past: the old person has time *in* him. But if this is so then middle age is the point at which the compression begins, and one feels that the present and future are being squeezed by the pressure from behind of the past. The reason the nostalgia of middle age, manifested, say, in listening again to music from one's youth, is so cloying and unhealthy is because such music brings back not lost time, but the world. But this was a world originally experienced simply as that: world. Now it is experienced as a *world in time*: a world steeped in the time that is *in* one. And that is a kind of psychological or spiritual contradiction. There is a way in which, phenomenologically speaking, human beings live in either space or time, but not both. The moment one realizes one lives in time is the moment in which the world begins to be lost to one, as if one were an empty vessel in the world which gradually becomes filled with a heavy liquid that disables one from moving. Hence the feeling common to middle age, which I have already mentioned, of having ground to a halt.

Because one's sense of youth, youth lost, is so deeply a matter of a mood lost, and because what one begins to lose in middle age is world or *space*, it is not surprising that a feeling for place – the place of one's youth – can easily become, in middle age, an object of fascination, even if it is horrified fascination. Places readily capture and retain moods that are there waiting for us to return to. They do so for all kinds of reasons, but one in particular is suggested by Marcel Proust. There are many memories that we have which become as it were exhausted or emptied or worn out precisely because they are so important to us. Other memories we have, but we do not notice their presence in us because we fail to see their importance. And precisely because we do not wear these memories out by our attention to them, they preserve much more of their original vigour, energy and significance for us. And memories of place tend to be very much like this. This is because we often take places to be backdrops for something *else* that is happening to us. And it is the something else that becomes the focus of the interest of our memory. The place, therefore, is in some ways better able to hold our memories for us, and this means that we can be unexpectedly overwhelmed by them when we return there. It is the very unimportance of the (memory of the) place when we were originally there that makes it so important now, when we return. The memories arise fresh in us, untrammelled by previous attention. Such, at any rate, is Proust's suggestion, which has the ring of truth about it.

I had myself grown up in the town P, and H, I discovered, still lived there, as he still does. Indeed, he still lives in the house in which he lived when he had the affair with my mother. I found this out very quickly, but I did not want simply to turn up at his house and walk in on his life, so it was some seven months after I found out about him that I finally went to his home and met him for the first time: for the first time, that is, since I had last seen him as my teacher when I was twelve years old.

I caught the train to the town and walked up High Street to H's house. I was completely overwhelmed by this dull, rather vulgar road, overwhelmed by the memory of the banal things that had happened to me there as a boy and young man: buying sweets and toys; helping my mother with the shopping; playing tennis in the near-by courts; and, later, drinking in pubs for the first time or catching the bus to visit a girlfriend. But I was also overwhelmed by what had *not* happened to me there, that is, that I could do all these things and *not* know that I was the son of H, who lived round the corner, and who might have been in High Street when I was. I had the sense that the world had known something profoundly intimate about me of which I was ignorant, as if anyone might have come up to me and told me the truth.

I had similar feelings after I left H – I had been with him about three hours and then suddenly felt a desperate need to get away – and walked past the house where I had been born and had grown up. The feeling I had was one of sickly longing, of an overwhelming and unbearable nostalgia. Everything seemed so small – literally physically small – and I felt as if I were walking around a model village, whose streets I had walked when I was myself physically much smaller and everything was, therefore, more in proportion.

Such feelings are, as I have said, typical of those one might well have in middle age for the places of one's youth. And it is as if one's identity is, in part at least, there, out there, in material world. H told me a strange thing: that when he is not in the town of P he feels as if he is not really alive. He said he had experienced this feeling for years. In one, literal sense, of course, what he said was not true, in that he would go on existing were he placed elsewhere. But I see no reason why someone might not have a feeling for a place so intense that he would lose much of the energy from his life if he no longer lived there.

We are dealing here with two different senses of what it is to be the same person. One, which we might call the *metaphysical* sense, is that in which I continue to be the same person even if some events intervene that radically change my understanding of what is of value or significance in life. I am, looked at from this point of view, the same person I was twenty or thirty years ago, and it is at least partly the narrative of my life that can be told that explains or shows why this is so. The other, which we might call the *spiritual* sense, although I do not mean that in any religious way, is an understanding of what it is to be the same person in which it is appropriate to say that I am not the same person I was twenty years ago: my sense of what is of importance or significance in life, my understanding of fundamental features of human life – birth, death, suffering, love, fulfilment, failure and so on – has changed so profoundly that it makes sense to say, indeed, that I am a quite different person from the one I was twenty years ago. This is a common way of speaking and comes naturally to us when we wish to record our feeling for some deep and important change in a person's understanding of life and what matters in it. In this latter sense, one's identity is, in part at least, out there in the world, so to speak: who we are is nourished by family, friends, lovers, colleagues, institutions, communities and so on. And I am suggesting that the material world – the world of places and their significance for us – plays a large role in this, a role that we tend only to see when it forces itself on us in the kind of way places do in the strange experiences of middle age. In this way, what H said about being in P records his feeling of attachment to place that gives him an understanding of who he is and what he is doing with his life.

One disquieting aspect of this sense of loss of the past and longing for it is a feeling of boredom with the present. I do not know how widespread this mood is in middle age, but I was struck by a corrosive sense of boredom, and Éric Deschavanne and Pierre-Henri Tavoillot suggest in their book on the philosophy of the different stages of life that such an emotion is widely shared among those in mid-life. They think of it as a kind of boredom in middle age like the boredom in the middle of the day experienced by the Desert Fathers, those Christian ascetics who, from about the third century on, withdrew to the desert to cultivate a highly rigorous spiritual discipline that ran the risk of leaving their inner life as barren as the desert which surrounded them. More exactly, it is like the acedia of midday, which, as Reinhard Kuhn writes, signified "lack of interest [and] became the recognized description for a condition of the soul characterized by torpor, dryness, and indifference" (*The Demon of Noontide*, 40). Deschavanne and Tavoillot write, *à propos* of middle age in the modern world:

> Everything takes place, in fact, as if the ancient symptom of "the demon of noontide", formerly the province of theological investigation (Psalm 91:6), had been generalized and democritized. For the Desert Fathers the problem was the temptation [to torpor] of noon that strikes anchorites during

the hottest part of the day. Far from leading to unbridled joy, the *demon of noontide* is the cause of "acedia", this melancholy mood tainted by a general disgust that distances both Christians and others in general from authentic spirituality. *What's the point?* is the key question of this "acedia". From this comes the double temptation of midday: regret for the morning (and its energy) and hope for the evening (with its serene calm). *(Philosophie des âges de la vie*, 42)

Be that as it may, it was as if my life had come to a standstill in a state of chronic boredom. I had achieved much of what I had wanted to achieve in life, yet I had made "the eternal error men make by imagining that happiness consists in the gratification of their wishes", as Tolstoy puts it in *Anna Karenina*. "What's the point?" became a pressing question for me, and in some moods I felt rather like Georg Büchner's Leonce:

The bees sit so lethargically on the flowers, the sunshine lies so lazily on the ground ... The things people do out of sheer boredom! They study out of boredom, they pray out of boredom, they fall in love, marry and have children out of boredom, and eventually die out of boredom and – that's the funny bit of it – all this with the most serious faces and without grasping why and, God knows, what for. All these heroes, geniuses, fools, saints, sinners, fathers are in the end nothing more than sophisticated idlers. – Why must I of all people know this? *(Leonce und Lena*, 162)

Somehow or other I could not rid myself of the thought that everything I did was something I was doing simply in order to kill time, and that this was true for others, even if they did not know it. And in such a mood I had the feeling that the main purpose of the human mind is to create for itself fetters with which it can torment itself, or turn itself into a torture chamber, as Nietzsche put the thought at many points in his work.

As I reflected on this boredom, reading philosophical, literary and psychoanalytic works in an effort to make sense of it, I began to feel that one reason I could find no way out of it was that I had no real idea what it was that could cure me of it. I started to feel that the boredom expressed a desire for something I knew not what, and that in a way nothing therefore could relieve me of it. A friend of mine told me of a time when he had passed through a period of intense boredom, and he said his feeling at that time was that life was absolutely wonderful *but that it was happening elsewhere.* This was also what I felt, along with the feeling, which was part of a sense of loss of the past, that if life had ever happened to me in all its wonder it was now all in the past. And so powerful was this feeling that it was as if my presence at anything was enough to render it boring. I had never before had this feeling in my life. Most fundamentally it was a feeling of boredom with myself. I was completely sick and tired of being the person I am, with my by now to me thoroughly familiar typical patterns of thought, emotion, inhibition, obsession, anxiety, need, longing, idiocy, weakness, self-deception and the rest.

I am sure that, as Pascal said, this boredom is one of the sources of religious belief. I do not mean that all who have faith are bored or have been bored. I mean that if human beings were not the kind of creatures to get bored in the way I have described then one of the roots of religious thought would be stripped from their condition. For the feeling of such chronic boredom is one of the inability of anything to satisfy one, but that is precisely something that, for example, Christianity claims: nothing here is ultimately fulfilling, and our true satisfaction lies elsewhere, in cleaving to God. Unfortunately, I think that diagnosis is right, but the putative cure a fantasy, although I do not say this lightly, since I once had a faith, and have spent most of my life struggling with the (im)possibility of belief. If religious faith is no longer possible, for me, then I certainly see this as a loss, although it also has its liberating side, and I feel, when I am in an upbeat mood, a terrific sense of relief that, for me, the baggage of Christianity is meaningless. When I hear people speaking of original sin, redemption, salvation, grace, God's outpouring and gracious love, Jesus as a personal friend, and so on, I sometimes feel repelled, sometimes indifferent, sometimes baffled. I am sure, however, that my experiences of middle age would have been easier, or, at any rate, would have made more sense, if I had had a faith, although that itself strikes me as suspicious, since I am now more than ever inclined to see something egotistical in faith, a kind of self-concern in which one is assured of one's own importance. For me, religious faith should be precisely such as to undermine that sense: it should take seriously Christ's injunction about giving all away, living in literal poverty, forgiving without limit, never judging and loving one's enemies. Some Christians have certainly sought to live that way, but I know that, given the person I am, I could not, which is one reason why I cannot believe.

The experience of boredom I am exploring is odd because one aspect of it was a sense that, even when I was able to find that this or that activity meant something to me, somehow none of it added up to anything. My condition was rather like that of the central figure in Chekov's "A Boring Story".

I think and think, and cannot think of anything. And however much I were to think and however far I were to scatter my thoughts, it is clear to me that the main thing, something very important, is lacking in my desires. In my partiality for science, in my desire to live, in my sitting here on a strange bed and in my longing to know myself, in all my thoughts, feelings and concepts about everything, there is no common link, there is nothing that might bind it together in one whole.

> Each thought and each feeling lives in me separately, and the most skilful analyst could not discover what is known as a ruling idea or what might be called the god of the living man in all my opinions of science, the theatre, literature, students, and all the pictures my imagination conjures up.
> And if that is not there, nothing is there.

("A Boring Story", 101)

This is a strange and disturbing spiritual state. It is not that one values nothing. It is rather that, even though there is much that one values, it remains somehow flat and empty, since it seems to have no essential connection with anything else that one values. That is one way of describing the boredom that afflicted me and, I think, afflicts many in middle age.

In a way, Heidegger puts his finger on something that is at issue here. In a series of lectures he gave in 1929 he explored the concept of boredom. Heidegger gives a categorization of three types of boredom. One kind he illustrates with an example, presumably from his own personal experience. He describes a dinner party. The food and conversation were good, and he felt no special need to leave early. Indeed, in a sense, he was quite content to be there. At the end of the evening he leaves, but on his way home he suddenly sees that he had been fantastically bored the whole evening. I think there is something right about this example. The boredom I felt was often one that only struck me after I left some event: a meal, drinks, a class I was teaching, a film, a play and so on. I felt that key here was a kind of restlessness, a sense that I wanted something from these activities that they simply could not, or did not, offer. I had no real idea what that was. But there was certainly a way in which I could not be fully absorbed or present in them, however valuable I found them, and I felt I had enormous amounts of intellectual energy spare that could not be absorbed because I could not settle to anything much for very long.

I said earlier that I had made the mistake of imagining that getting what I wanted in life would make me happy. And I did this even though I would have acknowledged much earlier that getting what I wanted was not likely to make me happy. I had believed that, but only theoretically, until reality caught up with me. Anyway, one could put the point another way, and more generally, as Judith Shklar put it: I discovered, gradually and painfully, that man has "a psychic structure ... [of a] self-contradictory and self-destructive character" (*Political Thought and Political Thinkers*, 143). These are the kinds of thought that mean nothing to a young person: it seems to make no sense whatever from a young person's perspective to think that getting what one wants is just the kind of thing that can make one unhappy. They are the fruit of the experience of life, and there is simply no way that they can be learnt or properly understood except through one's own experience.

This point about not being happy in getting what one wants is partly the point I made earlier that one does not understand the *meaning* of what is wanted until one gets it; and when one gets it, its meaning usually turns out to be quite other than expected. But it is also the old wisdom that one cannot sensibly aim for happiness; the best way to be happy is, largely anyway, to forget about happiness and get on with other things. It is also the point that human beings cannot – except, perhaps, after a great deal of spiritual self-disciplining – be content in resting in the moment. They need goals and aims, they need movement, even as they crave rest and peace. That is partly what Shklar meant in saying that human beings have a self-destructive and self-contradictory psychology.

This is essentially a tragic perspective on life. Or, rather, it is part of a perspective that, I believe, philosophers have generally sought to avoid facing. Thus I do not believe, as many, though not all, moral philosophers have wished to say, that the best bet for happiness in life is to be virtuous. This would only be true if human psychology were less chaotic, less given to aggression and more educable than is the case. It seems to me clear that some people might be happy by being virtuous, but others, indeed most, will find that being virtuous means they have to forgo some or many of the things they really would like to have, and I do not have mainly material things in mind, but forms of inner well-being, since morality often takes a punitive attitude towards much of the inner life. Further, a person's greed or envy or spite towards another might well stimulate him or her to produce much that is of great value; we know, for example, that many of those who have produced the greatest works of art have done so because they were in various ways motivated by envy of others who had already done so. As Auden said, "every artist knows that the sources of his art are what Yeats called 'the foul rag-and-bone shop of the heart', its lusts, its hatreds, it envies" (*Secondary Worlds*, 118). And at a more banal level, it is obvious that our capitalist society, which provides us with immense material plenty, depends on people's greed and vanity to stimulate them to buy. It seems to me also true, as Nietzsche suggested, that some of the moral notions with which we are most familiar, such as obligation ("you ought to do this") and blame ("it's your fault"), are at least partially motivated by things such as hatred and resentment, which morality itself rejects. In these various senses, vices are a necessary part of the total economy of the social world and of the human soul. Those who are truly good, like Christ, usually lose out because they will be exploited by those with fewer scruples: that is, by just about everyone else. And as I said at the outset, the contingencies and chance events in life are so widespread and so deep rooted that it can hardly be said that we are each of us in control of our life or have much by way of autonomy. Our lives drift; there is little we do to direct them. For all these reasons, I think that Orwell was right to say that, although most people get a fair amount of fun out of their life, the story of any life told honestly from the inside is a series of defeats. Rilke suggested this same thought in the first of his *Duino Elegies* from a general metaphysical and spiritual perspective when he wrote:

> and the knowing animals are indeed aware,
> that we are not very reliably at home
> in the interpreted world   (*Duineser Elegien: Erste Elegie*)

I think that human beings are largely a mess, and so is the life they lead.

***

In the Christian tradition, human beings are understood to be tainted with original sin. They are guilty by nature, regardless of anything specific they do. One way to put this would be to say that it is not *accidental* that they do things wrong: hurt each other; sacrifice others to their own interests; ignore the claims of need that others have on them. On this view, there is a kind of deep structural failure in the nature of human beings.

The doctrine of original sin is itself not entirely clear, since theologians disagree about its details and what it is supposed to entail. Moreover, it is quite unlikely that it could be established by argument as a metaphysical thesis, that is, as a claim about how human beings are and must therefore look at themselves if they are properly to understand what they are. Indeed, I suspect that no one is likely to accept an argument to the claim that there is some kind of structural failure in human beings unless he already has a sense of himself that he feels is well articulated by the idea. But that is to say that the argument cannot, after all, claim to establish a metaphysical thesis about human beings: it depends for any power or force it has on one's sense of one's spiritual condition, which will do the work in the argument.

Be that as it may, it seems to me that most of us are prone in middle age to have a sharpened sense of why it is that someone might think that human beings are fallen by nature or structurally flawed. This is because by the time we have reached middle age we are likely to be acutely aware of the ways in which we have hurt, and continue to hurt, others. This may be, and no doubt is, in part, a matter of our hurting others by being selfish, greedy or unkind. Sometimes it will have been thoughtlessness. But there is also a much subtler and more insidious way in which this is so. This is that simply the completely normal or natural efforts we make to establish ourselves in life and provide for our own needs often involve a disregard for others' interests and sometimes a thwarting of them as a kind of inevitable by-product of our self-concern. This comes out most clearly in close personal relationships and friendships, of course. But it is also apparent when people have to work closely together, or want their own share of limited goods. Simone Weil summed much of this up in her essay "Are We Struggling for Justice?" by remarking that, when we are engaged in our quotidian activities, we unthinkingly use others to achieve our ends without asking ourselves whether they have consented. Our only concern is with the success of the enterprise. "This is necessary. If it were otherwise", she writes, "things would not get done, and if things did not get done we would perish. But from this fact action is defiled by sacrilege" ("Luttons-nous pour la justice?", 47). Jacques Berthoud, in a discussion of Joseph Conrad's *The Secret Agent*, makes much the same point when, in describing a central theme of that book, he speaks of "the instinctive egoism of every positive assertion of individual life" (*Joseph Conrad*, 143). Indeed, much of Conrad's work can be thought of as an exploration of just this idea. It achieves profound expression in Mrs Gould's thought: "There was something inherent in the necessities of successful action which carried with it the moral degradation of the idea" (*Nostromo*, 521). Iris Murdoch spoke in this context of "the fat relentless ego" (*The Sovereignty of Good*, 52).

Even if one does not share such a view about human action as such, I think, nonetheless, as I have already intimated, that by middle age most people are likely to recognize that there are some ways in which they have hurt others that can never be made good. This is because we each of us have a lasting and probably permanent impact on the lives of some of those others. Their lives will have been touched by our own and their destiny will have been affected by their contact with us. It is inevitable that this will have been at least in part in some way deleterious. This may not be in overt material ways, although it may be, of course. It is more likely to be in terms of the impact one has had on another's sense of what is possible in life, of what he or she might do with his or her life, of what could make sense to him or her as a way of thinking and feeling about things. It goes without saying that I do not deny that one can have an enriching impact on others' sense of possibility and so on, but I think the more salient sense of things in middle age is likely to be one concerning the ways in which one has limited others' inner life in various ways.

I would not myself willingly speak of sin here on account of its theological or religious connotations, but from what I have said it will be clear why I feel the pull or temptation of such a way of speaking. And I certainly have an acute sense of the kind of guilt of which I have spoken, and this sense was crystallized for me, some eight years ago, by my undergoing, one afternoon, what I think of as a kind of inverse mystical experience: an experience that, in one way or another, has haunted me ever since. I suddenly saw myself as a relentlessly self-concerned, cold, shivering and emotionally dead self. This, indeed, was the source, or beginning, of that sense that I was devoid of love of which I spoke earlier. I was alone at the time, and felt a kind of inner emptiness that was unspeakably bleak. All I wanted to do was to fill up that gap, and I lay alone for about three hours listening to music – mainly Shostakovich's late quartets, which, in their bare, jagged and sparse minimalism, seemed both to express what I felt and yet also to provide some kind of solace.

Elliott Jaques published the paper "Death and the Mid-Life Crisis" in 1965, in which he introduced for the first time the concept of the mid-life crisis. He claimed that part of what is central to this idea is the working through of a depressive crisis in which one has to come to terms with the destructive and aggressive impulses, instincts and drives of the self, and be able to integrate them with the good, kind and gentle features of the self. Looked at from this point of view, what I experienced might be understood, in part at least, as a sudden realization of the destructive aspects of my inner life. But, in fact, I was not really struck by anything aggressive in me. What bothered me more were, as I have said, my completely normal forms of self-concern and self-protection that seemed so cold. Indeed, I had long been aware of the destructive side of my nature, mainly self-directed since adolescence, which had been with me from early childhood. But the sense of my inner coldness left me feeling desperately trapped in myself, as if I were suffocating.

This feeling of inner coldness was obviously connected with the craving for purity that I sketched earlier. I sometimes wonder whether this is not connected with my lack of faith.

I have often had the feeling that God *must* exist because only he could forgive me for being what I am. But since he does not, I cannot be forgiven and am condemned to a permanent sense of guilt. This sense of guilt is, however, not always a *feeling* of guilt. Sometimes it is rather the sense, as I said before, of being guilty in one's nature: that somehow guilt lies at the core of what one is. That may be experienced as a feeling of guilt, but need not be.

I do not know how typical such a sense of things is for most people in middle age. Perhaps many share with me a sense that what they are in the core of their being is guilty. But they might have different reasons for looking at things in this way. I spoke earlier of realizing in middle age the necessity of coping with who one is, with coming to terms with one's being the (kind of) person one is. And one aspect of this is brought out in Proust's phrase "the intermittences of the heart". By this Proust meant, roughly, that we are each of us a kind of bundle of different voices or persons: I am different as I write this book (and who that is, I am not sure) from the person I am with my friends, and that is again a different person from the one I am with my students or in a professional situation. Moreover, even in a personal relationship with one other person we are a multiplicity of voices, to all of which we cannot listen at any one time, and to some of which we cannot listen at all, without undermining the relationship, be it that of lovers, friends, siblings or whatever. These voices compete in us, and most of us spend a great deal of our lives trying to elevate one of them to the supreme voice, a voice that will drown out all the others, subdue them, remove them, so that we can become whole and complete. We do this basically for moral reasons – for reasons of getting on with others, for their sake and for our own – which shows one of the many ways in which morality requires falsehood of us. In any case, if one is the kind of person who has to cope with many different voices – and I think pretty much everyone is – then this can also engender a feeling of guilt, of some fracture deep inside that which one is. An example of the kind of thing I mean was provided by H. I asked him what kind of marriage he had had. Had he been happy? He was not sure if he had been happy, but he thought it had been a good marriage: solid, caring, orderly. But there was something lacking: a certain passion or emotional warmth. It was obvious that there was a voice in him that he had fairly systematically suppressed, except when he allowed it out in his relationship with my mother, who was everything other than solid and orderly, and was full of a kind of direct, restless energy. When H referred to his affair with her as a fiasco I felt hurt, since I experienced it as a kind of comment on me, although I am certain he did not mean it in that way. But it was also, I think, a rejection of one of his voices, and to some extent at least I experienced it as disingenuous, a denial of a reality about himself. That I can understand completely why he would wish to reject that voice does not alter my feeling in this regard.

Part of what is at issue here is the desire to be whole because one wishes to see the world as a whole, to find *the* right way of looking at it. There is an almost limitless supply of different perspectives on the world, of various political, moral, aesthetic and religious natures. There is something in the human mind that cannot stand this variety, and most of us long for some kind of stability here. We all find it hard to live with tensions between these different outlooks, even though – indeed, precisely because – we can be deeply attracted to them, depending on our mood, the weather, the books we are reading and the films we are seeing, our most recent or our deepest experiences, the period of our life in which we happen to find ourselves, and so on. In seeking to allow one voice to be dominant in us, we are seeking to allow only one view of the world to be the right or the most plausible view.

The attempt to find the single correct or right view on the world is, I think, doomed to failure: only by truncating the powers of the mind is it possible to be convinced that one has found such a view, although, of course, as I have already said, we are all of us willing to do violence to ourselves in this way to some extent or other, and, moreover, we have to in some ways, if only to get on with others. But if this dawns on one in middle age, it also dawns on one – it is a connected point – that all human beings are, by the time they get to middle age, if not before, in various ways deeply at odds with themselves. I once overheard a woman in a cafe say to a man that "the only normal people are those you don't know". That seems to me to be about right: we all of us carry around with us obsessions, anxieties, fears, neuroses, compulsions and inhibitions. As Adam Phillips says, "everyone is anxious all the time ... [and so] everyone needs reassurance, especially those who claim to loathe it ... [E]veryone is more confused than they seem" (*Going Sane*, 245). The human mind is fragmented, conflict-ridden, messy, recalcitrant and awkward. We find it hard to remember that others are like this, partly because we wish to conceal this from others because we are so ashamed of our being like this, and partly because our own inner states are so well known to us, and clearly so weird, that we imagine no one else could really be like this. But in a way, they are not weird, after all. That is partly my point. It is, in my view, one of the great features of friendship to be able to find consolation for being like this in seeing that another is like this too, for it is our friends that will allow us to see this in them, just as we allow our friends to see this in us. At any rate, that is my basic view of friendship: a kind of relationship in which one allows the other as much as possible to be just as he is without requiring him to be otherwise.

But in fact there is, in my view, not only a certain fear, perhaps, but also a tremendous freedom in accepting that there is no single right view on life: it gives a profound sense of possibility and opportunity in thought and feeling. This is an inner freedom from constraint. There is, that is to say, less to *defend* if one accepts that one's own view is not the right view, the correct view, if one can accept that we are all doing our best to make the best of a bad job and that, in a way, no one, really, knows anything more than anyone else about what finally matters. And there is thus an absence of what would otherwise be there: the need, as it were, to be vigilant against threats to what one takes to be the truth and thus a kind of inner tension on the look-out for – or, at any rate, reactive in the face of – the disturbing thoughts of others.

***

The most extreme response to the sense that one is a mess is suicide. Albert Camus, in his *The Myth of Sisyphus*, flatly asserts that all healthy human beings have thought about their own suicide (*Le Mythe de Sisyphe*, 20). Even if he is right, this will not be, I assume, in the sense of contemplating actually doing it. Nonetheless, when

I learnt the truth about H I felt such a horrible sense of revulsion from myself and from my life that I thought again, as I have at times in my life, about what the point was of going on.

According to Camus, the question of suicide is the first and most important philosophical question, and it is, indeed, a question that one cannot help answering. For if one never thinks about whether it is worth going on, then one has answered the question, since never to have considered taking one's life is to have judged that life is worth going on with.

G. K. Chesterton once remarked that the man who kills another man, kills one man; the man who kills himself kills all men: he wipes out the world (*Orthodoxy*, 65). Chesterton intended, in saying this, I think, to claim that anyone who kills himself shows an ingratitude for life, since he rejects the world in its entirety. Kant expressed a similar thought when he claimed that the person who takes his own life leaves the world as though it were a smoke-filled room (*Lectures on Ethics*, 148, 369).

There is clearly something right about the Chesterton–Kant view. In Arthur Schnitzler's short story "Lieutenant Gustl", a masterpiece of psychological observation and insight, the eponymous hero – or, rather, anti-hero – is slighted after a concert in the crush of people at the cloakroom by a civilian, a baker, who refuses to give way before Gustl's higher social standing. Gustl is, according to the mores of social form prevailing at that time and place – *fin-de-siècle* Vienna – profoundly dishonoured. He cannot challenge the baker to a duel, and, in any case, the baker's social standing makes him "*satisfaktionsunfähig*": incapable of giving the officer satisfaction in this regard. Gustl wanders the streets of Vienna all night, and comes to the conclusion that his only way out is suicide. And he does so because his entire personality is governed by the clichés and rhetoric of military life of a certain kind. Schnitzler wants us to understand that he is simply too small of soul, too narrow in outlook, too thoughtless, to grasp the limitations of his own way of life and of his own thoughts and feelings. He is thus incapable of seeing the absurdity and childishness of his desire for death. And I think that there is in him – although he could not see this – a kind of ingratitude, an incapacity to see that life is so much more than the present form it takes for him, that is, his being as an officer, and his difficulties over being slighted.

But Gustl's situation is not the same as that of all those who consider suicide. His way of thinking of the issue does not capture the spirit of all those who contemplate such action. Indeed, I think that there can be cases where someone commits suicide out of a certain kind of fidelity to life; I am thinking of those, for example, who, wracked by pain and suffering, feel that there is an indignity and pointlessness about their lives and choose to end things. No doubt such people can commit suicide in the spirit of a denial of life, but it is far from clear why this should always be assumed to be so. They might do so, paradoxical as this may sound, in a spirit of affirmation of life.

I find it hard to think one could arrive at middle age and not have contemplated what the point is of going on. In one way, this feeling of mine is clearly mistaken, since there are many who have not thought about such things. But it perhaps belongs to an understanding of middle age to see that this is the time of life when, if such thoughts are likely to come to one at all, they will strike, barring irremediable illness and the like at other times of one's life. For, as I have been suggesting in many ways, by middle age one will have grasped more clearly the ways in which one's encounter with oneself and the world is defective or unsatisfactory. In my case, a sense of that has accompanied me throughout my life. Aristotle suggested that the beginnings of philosophy lie in a sense of wonder at the world. I became a philosopher mainly on account of my sense of the difficulty of the world, and most of my philosophical work – including this book – has involved, among other things, an attempt to make sense of the difficulty of the world, partly by trying to find it less difficult than I naturally find it, and partly by adjusting or moderating my sense of what the difficulty in life is.

This point about suicide, which, I am suggesting, is bound up with the experience of middle age, comes out clearly in Tolstoy's discussion of his crisis of mid-life. Having described the way in which he felt his life to have ground to a halt, which left him no answer to the question of why he was doing what he was doing with his life, he first sums up his experience and then goes on to discuss his attitude towards suicide:

> My life came to a standstill. I could breathe, eat, drink and sleep and I could not help breathing, eating, drinking and sleeping; but there was no life in me because I had no desires whose gratification I would have deemed it reasonable to fulfil. If I wanted something I knew in advance that whether or not I satisfied my desire nothing would come of it.
>
> Life had grown hateful to me, and some insuperable force was leading me to seek deliverance from it by whatever means. I could not say that I wanted to kill myself. The force beckoning me away from life was a more powerful, complete and overall desire. It was a force similar to my striving after life, only it was going in the other direction. I fought as hard as I could against life. The thought of suicide now came to me as naturally as thoughts of improving my life had previously come to me. This idea was so attractive to me that I had to use cunning against myself in order to avoid carrying it out too hastily. I did not want to rush, simply because I wanted to make every effort to unravel the matter. I told myself that if I could not unravel the matter now, I still had time to do so. And it was at this time that I, a fortunate man, removed a rope from my room where I undressed every night alone, lest I hang myself from the beam between the cupboards; and I gave up taking a rifle with me on hunting trips so as not to be

tempted to end my life in such an all too easy fashion. I myself did not know what I wanted. I was afraid of life and strove against it, yet I still hoped for something from it.

(*A Confession*, 30)

Among the many striking things here is the way that Tolstoy brings out how he was beguiled by the thought of his own suicide, and yet in some sense did not seriously think of ending his own life. Had he ended his life it would have been almost by accident. He did not want to kill himself, and yet somehow could find no clear reason why he should not do it.

It is also striking that Tolstoy says that the force which was pulling him away from life "was a more powerful, complete and overall desire" than any desire to take his own life. This is odd and extremely interesting, since one might have thought that there could not be a desire taking one from life stronger than the desire to kill oneself. How could there be stronger desire away from life than that?

Here is a suggestion. Schopenhauer claimed that there is a kind of contradiction in suicide: on the one hand, suicide expresses a desire to negate one's own will, by putting an end to one's willing completely through death; on the other hand, it involves a very profound and powerful expression of one's will. In some sense then there exists a kind of self-refuting quality about suicide, since in killing oneself one would be asserting a fundamental feature of one's life as an active agent; namely, one's will. Suicide is, in a way, thus a kind of weird active engagement for and on behalf of life. But in Tolstoy's case, the desire for suicide did not, in fact, at least in some straightforward sense, involve such an engagement. On the contrary, it was driven more by apathy and was, indeed, as he himself says, not really a desire for death so much as an indifference to life. Hence, oddly enough, his apathy was a more powerful motive away from life and than any active searching for death could have been. Moreover, Tolstoy was influenced by Schopenhauer, so it may well have been natural for him to express himself, implicitly at any rate, in Schopenhauerian terms.

Part of what these thoughts about suicide articulate is what Christopher Ricks has called a "counter-truth": a truth, that is, counter to the fact that "[m]ost people most of the time want to live for ever"; namely, "that, on occasion and more moodily, we want oblivion, extinction, irreversible loss of consciousness". He goes on to say that this counter-truth:

> is insufficiently, or is mostly prophylactically, rendered by literature. Authorities, sacred and secular, do not care for the thought; they do not want you to want to be dead. Except, perhaps, as a martyr, and even this they have their doubts about.
>
> Yet who would maintain, through thick and thin, that the energy which is consciousness is eternal delight? Consciousness does not have to be pained to be a burden or to be a perturbation of mind in endless prospect.
>
> (*Beckett's Dying Words*, 1)

Ricks is surely right. As Améry pointed out, the authorities leave you alone to make of your life what you will, but when they think you might want to die they suddenly step in and do all they can to keep you going. There is clearly something here that one is not *allowed* to think.

Perhaps one is forbidden such thoughts partly because they seem to go clean against something that is so deeply embedded in each of us, that is, that we do, as Ricks says, most of the time want to live forever. Yet to emphasize this in the wrong way is simply to fail to acknowledge Ricks's counter-truth, to load the dice against those who say what they are not allowed to say; namely, that they sometimes want something very far from going on forever. But that thought stands at the start – or pretty much – of Western culture in the comment made by the chorus in Sophocles' *Oedipus at Colonus* that the best luck one can have is not to be born at all, but that, once born, the best thing is to die soon. Apparently, so Ricks tells us, Thomas Hardy genuinely wished he had never been born.

But if one is not allowed to think such thoughts then this will be because one has internalized what the authorities want. In my case, the central form of that is the feeling that I ought to be grateful for life: that I ought to see life as a gift. It is a thought that I find burdensome; being haunted by the idea that I ought to see life as a gift, I am less able to do so. I think I received the idea that life should be viewed in a spirit of gratitude partly from my education in Christian schools, and partly from my mother, who forbade feelings such as those of boredom, depression and listlessness even as she did more than her fair share in encouraging them in those around her. Be that as it may, thoughts about my non-existence have for me today a peculiarly vertiginous quality since my mother told me that, when K discovered that she was pregnant by H, he tried to persuade her to have an abortion. She was appalled, I think, by the fact that I could, and can, understand why he wanted this: I do not take it as any mark against his character that he wanted her to abort the child she was carrying. And that is so even though I am, in general, opposed to abortion, although I can well see that there are cases in which any humane person will understand why someone wants, or needs, to be a free of a pregnancy in this way. When I think about the fact that I might have been aborted – and there are many, of course, of whom this is true, although they may, I suppose, not know this about themselves since it is not the kind of thing parents like to advertise to their children – I find the thought baffling. In part this is a familiar difficulty about being unable to conceive one's own nothingness. But in part it is also the sense that, in one way, it would not have made any difference if I had never existed in the first place, and therefore would not really make any difference if I now ceased to exist: the world would happily go on its way without me.

In any case, if you have a sense of life as difficult, then it must be that you are operating according to some image, however implicit, of a life that is not difficult: some life, or way of life, that would answer to your expectations. For Tolstoy that was, as he came to find out, a life of asceticism and what he interpreted as primitive Christianity. In an interesting exploration of such matters, Adorno wrote: "Anyone who died old and in the consciousness of seemingly blameless success, would secretly be the model schoolboy who reels off all life's stages without gaps or omissions, an invisible satchel on his back" (*Minima Moralia*, 81). And in a discussion of Jeremy Bentham, John Stuart Mill, who admired Bentham very much, said he:

> had little experience. He had neither internal experience nor external; the quiet, even tenor of his life, and his healthiness of mind, conspired to exclude him from both. He never knew prosperity and adversity, passion or satiety: he never knew the experiences which sickness gives; he lived from child-hood to the age of eighty-five in boyish health. He knew no dejection, no heaviness of heart. He never felt life a sore and weary burthen. He was a boy to the last. Self-consciousness, that dæmon of the men of genius of our time ... and to which this age owes so much of both its cheerful and its mournful wisdom, never was awakened in him. How much of human nature slumbered in him he knew not, neither can we know. He had never been made alive to the unseen influences which were acting on himself, nor consequently on his fellow-creatures.   (*Mill on Bentham and Coleridge*, 62–3)

Thinking about Adorno's general comments together with Mill's specific remarks on Bentham helps to remind us of the fact that it is extremely unclear just what we are doing when we think of certain things in our life as successes – or failures. There is a very interesting spiritual dilemma here, exemplified in the case of Nietzsche. He certainly gave up relatively early in his life the idea of leading a life that might be wholly successful, in whatever way he, or we, might understand that. He knew life would contain unwanted pain and suffering and failure. But from this willingness to be open to failure, he insisted on trying to find another way to think of his life as immune to such. He wanted to be able to look the mistakes in the eye and affirm them, which would itself stop them being mistakes. In other words, his insistence that life is full of failures was supposed to be something so thoroughly accepted and seen for what it is that there would, after all, be no failures in his life. What he could not accept was that there were parts of his life that were simply through and through forms of mistake: of waste or pointless activity. This is, of course, not a criticism of him. It is rather a way of highlighting the immense difficulty in accepting failure in life, for accepting it can be a form of interpreting it as not being a failure after all. Adorno's very insistence on the importance of seeing life as being full of gaps is, after all, in one sense, a way of closing the gaps. To live with failure *as* failure – to live with it, that is, without its crippling one spiritually, psychologically, emotionally – seems, in a way, impossible. As Shakespeare expresses it:

[T]he worst is not
So long as we can say "This is the worst".
(*King Lear*, IV.i.27–8)

In any case, Nietzsche, in a famous passage in *The Gay Science*, devised a kind of test for one's attitudes to one's failures:

The greatest weight – What, if one day or night a demon were to steal into your loneliest loneliness and say to you: "This life as you now live it and have lived it, you will have to live once more and countless times more; and there will be nothing new in it, but every pain and every joy and every thought and sigh and everything indescribably small and great in your life will have to return to you, all in the same succession and sequence – even this spider and this moonlight between the trees, and even this moment and I myself. The eternal hourglass of existence is turned upside down again and again, and you with it, speck of dust!" Would you not throw yourself down and gnash your teeth and curse the demon who spoke in this way? Or have you ever experienced a tremendous moment when you would have answered him: "You are a god and never have I heard anything more divine!" If this thought gained possession of you, it would transform you as you are or perhaps crush you. The question in each and every thing, "Do you desire this once more and countless times more?" would lie upon your actions as the greatest weight. Or how well disposed would you have to become to yourself and to life *to crave nothing more fervently* than this ultimate eternal confirmation and seal?   (*Die fröhliche Wissenschaft*, §341)

This passage has been the subject of a great deal of discussion by commentators on Nietzsche. No one is quite sure what to make of it, and it may be that the thought is incoherent. But something like the following seems to be what Nietzsche intended. In one way the passage suggests an attitude towards the past that you are now asked to take: you are asked whether you would be willing to live that past again, just as it was. That would involve, Nietzsche thinks, an attitude to your failures, namely, that they would no longer be seen as failures. And that leads to the kinds of problems I have already discussed. In another way, the passage looks forward to the future: suppose I ask myself in each thing I do whether I would be willing to do it again and again to eternity. Then I would certainly think a great deal harder about many of my deeds and actions than I do already. For sure, there are plenty of things I do, and would willingly do, again and again because, although boring in the extreme, they are means to something else that I want to do for its own sake. Going shopping is one example, since, although I dislike doing this, I do it because otherwise I would have nothing to eat. But there are other things that seem not to fall into this category. If I think, for example, of the shameful, hurtful, mean-spirited things I have done that have ruined days for myself and others, then I could not will that I do these again and again, and that gives me, right now, the sense that I do not want to destroy any time whatever again in my life by doing those things. Nietzsche's test forces me to try to think reflectively about what I am now going to do with my life and so actively avoid those things that I know to be destructive. But, of course, I know that I shall not entirely be able to avoid acting in this way, because I know that doing such is just part of what life is.

We are back with the idea of human beings' guilty condition, since what I have just articulated is a sense of my knowledge that I will do mean and unkind things, will spoil things for myself and others. And you know this of yourself too. The feeling of guilt here is in part the experience of being cut off from life, being in some way life-denying. As Franz Kafka put it in one of his so-called Zürau aphorisms, we are "sinful ... because we have not yet eaten of the Tree of Life" (*Zürauer Aphorismen*, no. 83). It seems, Kafka is saying, that we find it more or less impossible to enter a kind a fullness of existence.

There are many possible routes into that thought; here is one. In the Preface to his *Lyrical Ballads*, Wordsworth speaks of "the grand elementary principle of pleasure", which he thinks of as "the native and naked dignity of man". It is, he says, the principle by which "he [man] knows, and feels, and lives, and moves" (Preface to *Lyrical Ballads*, 173). The thought is in part blasphemous since it echoes, and subverts, St Paul's claim that in God "we live, and move, and have our being" (Acts 17:28). The concept of pleasure has a bad press among philosophers: it stood at the centre of Bentham's well-meaning but shallow theory of utilitarianism, which directs us to act in such a way as always to maximize the pleasure of those affected by our action. For Bentham, pleasure seemed pretty much to be a sensation, which hardly is the case when one thinks of, say, the pleasure of listening to Bach or being excited by a philosophical idea. Moreover, Bentham seriously suggested that all pleasures could be related on a numerical scale such that listening to Bach would give to such and such a person a certain number of units of pleasure, eating ice cream would give him a certain other number of units of the same, and then he could act in such a way as to maximize the units of pleasure by choosing the one or the other activity. It is hardly surprising that Mill thought of Bentham as being like a boy, and it was against the reductiveness of Bentham's theory that Mill tried to distinguish qualities of pleasure, suggesting that, to use the same example, listening to Bach gives a greater *quality* of pleasure than does eating ice cream. But Mill remained caught in the toils of utilitarianism's shallowness, and the concept of pleasure has since then been too closely associated with that theory's way of looking at things for philosophers who are rightly contemptuous of utilitarianism to take it very seriously. But Wordsworth's comments about pleasure are so arresting, and so far from a utilitarian conception of it, that it is worth looking a little more closely at what he says.

I myself would wish to connect the idea that pleasure constitutes (a central part of?) the dignity of man to Ecclesiastes' thought that all is vanity and vexation of spirit. In the light of that latter thought the taking of pleasure can, I think, be seen as a mark of man's dignity. This is because Ecclesiastes' thought will only make sense if one really grasps in one's heart the emptiness – the vanity – of more or less all of life: the endless struggle both with oneself and others for prestige, honour, wealth, influence, fame and so on.

One could think of this as the comedy of human existence. And, I think, when one is struck by this thought one can see why the concept of pleasure can offer so much for human dignity, for in the light of such a thought ordinary activities from which we can take so much pleasure – eating, sleeping, lying vacantly in the summer grass, reading a poem, listening to a song, smoking a cigarette – can provide pleasure that is not simply nice or agreeable, but deeply *noble*.

I think this is (one reason) why Wordsworth speaks of the *naked* dignity of man: it is incredibly hard to retain that sense of pleasure. In fact, it is not simply hard to do so, but impossible. I do not mean that one cannot have that sense from time to time. I mean that it is impossible to retain it for any extended period of time. This is not simply on account of the exigencies of life: the need to earn a living, to do something to secure one's future and so on. It is also, and more importantly, because human beings are so constituted that there is no conceiving of them without conflict and tension in their lives. For there seems really to be no way in which we can conceive of a human being who would not be distinguished by having an inner life – a life of desire, need, wish, hope, longing and so on – that might or might not be expressed outwardly, in the body or in action, an inner life that might come apart from external mani-festation. And that is enough to generate conflict or tension, even if only at a rudimentary level, since it directly introduces notions such as inhibition, suppression, repression, the checking of desire and so on. For the point about pleasure from the perspective under consideration is that it involves precisely an absence of that conflict: in such pleasure, the self rests in the moment and in its activity, transparent, so to speak, to, and through to, the world in which it is engaged. There is here no suppression or repression, no checking of desire or need. Hence, Wordsworth speaks of the *naked* dignity: man would have to be psychologically and spiritually naked to be able to live in the pleasure in question.

In any case, I think that one of the things one discovers in middle age is the importance and dignity of *pleasure* in life. Much of the first half of life is spent, as mine was, trying to establish oneself, achieve some material well-being and security, a place in the working world, and so on. I think many people go through this process and then, in middle age, have the sense of having missed out on something crucial in life. Hence, Nietzsche's thought about only doing now whatever one can will to do again and again to eternity can easily take the form of a kind of urgency about enjoying simple pleasures of the kind I mentioned earlier, which is why Nietzsche, in middle age, mocked those who worry about the existence of God, the nature and meaning of morality, and so on, instead of learning to enjoy the small pleasures of life.

From one perspective, Nietzsche's life was an exemplary success: he was, in one way or another, influential on just about every significant cultural movement of the twentieth century; his life and work are discussed at endless length by philosophers, psychoanalysts, literary and cultural critics and others; and he is revered as a master of the German language, one of its most formative influences, along with Luther and Goethe. Yet, he was lonely, unhappy and he experienced very little pleasure in life, partly because he suffered from terrible ill health. He almost certainly never spent a night with the comfort of a naked woman next to him in bed, as Stefan Zweig put his feeling for Nietzsche's loneliness in the essay on him in his book *The Struggle with the Demon*, could drink almost no alcohol without becoming ill, suffered appalling migraines and often had to spend days in bed, had dreadful eyesight and so on. So, in another way, his life was an exemplary failure.

I doubt that it makes much sense to try to sum up his life as overall a success or a failure. It was simply what it was: looked at in one way a success, in another a failure. Many lives are like this: very roughly speaking, from the inside a failure, from the outside a success, or *vice versa*. And there is no such thing as the *one* correct narrative of a life, the narrative that will reveal whether it has overall been one or the other. Sometimes the most valuable friends and those who can otherwise give most are those whose lives are miserable from the inside. Johnson was like this; his life was deeply wretched, but he gave so much to his friends, and was such a source of enrichment for them, that they simply could hardly imagine their lives without him. "He has made a chasm, which not only nothing can fill up, but which *nothing has a tendency to fill up*", Bate tells us one of his friends wrote when Johnson died. "Johnson is dead. – Let us go the next best: There is nobody" (*Samuel Johnson*, 599).

***

In a marvellous essay on Dostoyevsky, one of his *Three Masters* essays (the others are on Balzac and Dickens), Zweig wrote:

> Wherever one digs more deeply into Dostoyevsky's work there roars everywhere as the deepest source this wholly primitive, almost vegetative fanatical craving for life, this feeling for existence, this wholly primordial craving, not concerned about happiness or suffering – which are mere individual forms of life, valuations, distinctions – but rather about the wholly undifferentiated desire that one feels when one breathes.
>
> (*Drei Meister*, 130)

In Freudian terms, Zweig sees in Dostoyevsky an honesty about the longing for plenitude that haunts all of us throughout life in various ways and which becomes especially pressing in middle age, for then one most acutely realizes the absolute hopelessness of the thought that it will ever be satisfied. The desire in question is, roughly speaking, the desire for a fullness of existence – of emotional and physical life – that was the infant's possession but lost at birth, when ejected into a world that can never, and could never, minister to it sufficiently.

Some of our most basic desires can assume the weight of the hope for a final and consoling plenitude: sexual desire is one, which is partly why Jean Laplanche spoke of the "traumatic burden of sexuality". When a desire assumes such a form, part of what is going on is the fantasy that it could be satisfied in such a way as to end it – or even all desire – for good. Phillips, for example, speaks of a boy who was "excessively greedy". The boy said to him: "If I eat everything I won't have to eat anymore". Phillips comments:

> This could have meant several things, but for him it meant then that if he could eat everything he would no longer need to be hungry. One magical solution to the problem of having been tantalized is to have no desire. For this boy greed was, among other things, an attack on the desiring part of the self, a wish to get to the end of his appetite and finish with it once and for all. Part of the total fantasy of greed is always the attempt to eat up one's own appetite.
>
> (*On Kissing, Tickling and Being Bored*, 74)

Simon Critchley has suggested in his book *On Humour* that, in the face of the desire for plenitude, we have to be able to laugh at ourselves, to find ourselves ridiculous: laughter and smiling – at oneself – are forms of anti-depressant. It is a magnificent thought, and I have no doubt that he is right. In a sense, as I understand the idea, part of what is at issue here is a kind of urbanity. And perhaps this is best seen in the example of Montaigne, who is, as Zweig said in another of his great essays, *the* thinker of middle age. As Zweig puts it:

> That one only knows how to honour Montaigne's wisdom and greatness when one has been tested by the experience of life is something I experienced for myself. When I first, at the age

of twenty, took up his *Essays* – that single book in which he has left himself to us – I hardly knew, to be honest, what to make of it … In order to understand Montaigne's art of living and wisdom of life, as well as to understand his struggle for his own self as the most crucial struggle in the world of thought, I had to have experiences something like Montaigne's own … I too had to feel that my hopes, experiences, expectations and enthusiasms had been chased out of me with a whip until I had reached a point where I had nothing more to defend but my naked self, my unique and irretrievable life. Only in a fraternity of such fate did Montaigne first become a brother, helper, comforter and friend … *(Montaigne*, 5–6)

Central to Montaigne's urbanity is not simply what he says, but the way in which he says it: his manner or style. There is throughout Montaigne's writing a certain coolness of manner, a kind of capacious ability to accept himself and take an endless interest in the inventiveness and varieties of human experience. Further, he had an abhorrence of dogma and metaphysical speculation, believing that these lead to conflict and cannot, in any case, seriously help with the problems of everyday, practical life. And he had an unhurried acceptance of the body and its pleasures, indeed a recognition that the body plays a very great role in one's thinking, as do climate and the physical and material environment generally.

Clearly Montaigne's cool moderation is hardly likely to be the kind of thing that appeals to youth. But then, as Conrad said, to be insolent, is the right of youth: "its necessity; it has got to assert itself, and all assertion in this world of doubts is a defiance, is an insolence" (*Lord Jim*, 236). What Montaigne found interesting was something that was never far from Conrad's mind:

And besides, the last word is not said … Are not our lives too short for that full utterance which through all our stammerings is of course our only and abiding intention? I have given up expecting those last words, whose ring, if they could only be pronounced, would shake both heaven and earth. There is never time to say our last word – the last word of our love, of our desire, faith, remorse, submission, revolt. (*Lord Jim*, 225)

But just as there is not enough time to say our last word, there is never enough time to hear the last word from others. One's own mind, however much it might be needed by another, is not some blank recipient of what he or she has to say, and despite one's best efforts what one offers to others can never be what they want, something that accepts their understanding of themselves yet is a mind of its own. Or perhaps the only mind like that is God's, which is not only omniscient but also infinitely forgiving. Another's need of one can in that sense never be satisfied, and since one might need the other's need of one this creates a further sense – infinitely extendable – of the inability either to say or hear the final word. This would remain so even if we were immortal: it is simply part of what we are and of what life is.

Montaigne was able to bear these frustrations, I have suggested, not simply on account of what he thought, which involved the full development of his expansive sensibility, but because of the way he thought it, that is, his style. And he was well aware of this:

The man who says what is true can act as foolishly as the one who says what is untrue: we are talking about the way you say it not what you say. My humour is to consider the form as much as the substance ... Every day I spend time reading my authors, not caring about their learning, looking not for their subject-matter but how they handle it; just as I go in pursuit of discussions with a celebrated mind not to be taught by it but to get to know it.

("On the Art of Conversation", in *The Complete Essays*, 1051)

I am reminded by this passage of Arendt's wonderful comment that "truly human dialogue differs from mere talk or even discussion in that it is entirely permeated by pleasure in the other person and what he says. It is tuned to the key of gladness" ("On Humanity in Dark Times", 15). And a good example of Montaigne's own style comes – appropriately enough – in his discussion of vanity:

> Perhaps there is no more manifest vanity than writing so vainly about it ... Anyone can see that I have set out on a road along which I shall travel without toil and without ceasing as long as the world has ink and paper. I cannot give an account of my life by my actions: Fortune has placed them too low for that; so I do so by my thoughts. Thus did a nobleman I once knew reveal his life only by the workings of his bowels: at home he paraded before you a series of seven or eight days' chamber-pots. He thought about them, talked about them: for him any other topic stank. Here (a little more decorously) you have the droppings of an old mind, sometimes hard, sometimes squittery, but always ill-digested.   ("On Vanity", in *The Complete Essays*, 1070)

Montaigne was confronting the problem of how to be stoical about the fact that we will simply never get all we want or need because we are possessed of a limitless desire for plenitude, and yet at the same time not allow that to render us melancholy and enervated. Montaigne was able to accept his melancholy for what it was and yet find a way past it through his humour. In a way, what we need to recover in middle age in order to deal with it is a certain capacity to play.

One of Montaigne's ways of playing – given that he was a man who had retired from public life in order to think and write – is to be found in his play with ideas. Part of this is the ability to resist the strong temptation we all have to seek to "talk for victory", as Johnson put it: to believe that one has achieved something worthwhile in having silenced another's objections to one's own point of view. In a very great essay on conversation, Michael Oakeshott, without directly referring to him, captured something of the spirit of things for which Johnson was aiming – or hoping:

> In a conversation the participants are not engaged in an inquiry or a debate; there is no "truth" to be discovered, no proposition to be proved, no conclusion sought. They are not concerned to inform, to persuade, or to refute one another .... Of course, a conversation may have passages of argument and a speaker is not forbidden to be demonstrative; but reasoning is neither sovereign nor alone, and the conversation itself does not compose an argument ... In conversation ... [t]houghts of different species take wing and play round one another, responding to each other's movements and provoking one another to fresh exertions. Nobody asks where they have come from or on what authority they are present; nobody cares what will become of them when they have played their part. There is no symposiarch or arbiter, not even a doorkeeper to examine credentials. Every entrant is taken at its face-value and everything is permitted which can get itself accepted into the flow of speculation. And voices which speak in conversation do not compose a hierarchy. Conversation is not an enterprise designed to yield an extrinsic profit, a contest where a winner gets a prize, nor is it an activity of exegesis; it is an unrehearsed intellectual adventure. It is with conversation as with gambling, its significance lies neither in winning nor in losing, but in wagering.
>
> ("The Voice of Poetry in the Conversation
> of Mankind", 489–90)

A complementary view of conversation that emphasizes even more directly than Oakeshott does the playful side of such discourse is offered by Leon Kass.

Though conversation permits disagreements, it is in spirit different from argument. Argument is earnest and seriously bent on victory or conversion ... A conversation is built by the free play of the mind, out of information, stories, experiences and opinions contributed by the participants, each of whom is open to the already contributed speeches, and to the souls, of the contributing speakers ... Though wit is welcome, indeed, prized, in such conversation, it is not a contest of wit but a "game" in which there are no losers ... Because our interest is in both the speakers and the speeches, conversation enables us to taste, indeed to savor, the souls of our fellow [partners in conversation] – ... that wonderful side of the soul at play, when it is unself-consciously and immediately being its open, companionable, and responsive self ... Conversation is a special, playful perfection of speaking ...

(*The Hungry Soul*, 171, 173)

Both Oakeshott and Kass distinguish argument from conversation. However, in doing so they fail to see something that Montaigne stressed. This is that we very often suppose that we have discovered the truth in some area – say, about a moral problem, or about a judgement of aesthetic worth – and think, therefore, that we can offer an argument such that all others who hear and follow it ought to agree with us. But, Montaigne thinks, this is an illusion: what we think of as the truth is, at best, really only our individual truth, and derives its peculiar power over us from, for example, our personal experiences or some way in which it moves or excites us. Others who have not had these experiences (and so on) do not find the argument convincing, even if they can see why we accept it. They actually treat our view as a move in a conversation and as less powerful as a force for conversion or victory than we think it is. But the same applies, for us, to their relation to their own view. So, on Montaigne's view, argument is actually a debased or dishonest form of conversation: it is one thing pretending to be something else. Hence for Montaigne it is central to the wisdom of life to bear this in mind and cultivate a cheerful scepticism about one's own views and opinions.

Of course, it remains an ideal to give up argument in the sense in which Oakeshott and Kass speak of it and to seek always for a style of thought, like Montaigne's, which is conversational. This is an ideal because our own view will often seem to us to be the correct view with which others ought to agree, and so we will often need to remind ourselves that, on account of the fallibility, weakness and unclarities of our own thought, this is not so. But the attempt to achieve such an ideal is, in my view, not only necessary as a matter of honesty, but is also key both to avoiding a kind of intolerance and fanaticism in thought and to finding a way of thinking that is wise, as Montaigne's is, because it is playful.

***

I have not spoken here of what must be central to many people's experience of middle age; namely, that of having their own children. I have not done so since I am not a parent. But I can say something about the meaning of having no children by the time one is in middle age. There are increasing numbers of people who are in this position, so what I say on this issue might resonate with them. And it might also be of relevance to those with children, since their experience is bound to be, in some ways, complementary to my own.

When I was young – probably no more than eight or nine years old – I remember that I had as a kind of dawning moment of self-knowledge the thought that I would not have children. Looking back now this seems a wholly absurd thought, since it is one whose meaning cannot be grasped by so young a child. Nonetheless, I have not since had children, and have never seriously felt the desire to do so. I suppose that it is inevitable that I link my childhood thought with my own experiences when I was a child. The house I grew up in was extremely violent, and I witnessed many scenes of physical and verbal abuse between K and my mother. My image of domestic life was in this sense negative. I myself suffered dreadful, and regular, outbreaks of hysterical anger, after which I always underwent intensely painful bouts of remorse, and during which I felt myself to be possessed of, or by, two selves, one raging out of control, the other ice cold, observing what was happening to the other self and able to check its behaviour if things went too far. Such an experience in childhood is not, I think, so very unusual. At least, this is suggested by Edmund Gosse. He relates an incident where he behaved badly, damaging a fountain his father had constructed in the garden, and greatly feared his father's wrath. But his father did not suspect that his son was responsible, the blame falling on some workmen, and he, the young Gosse, closed himself around his secret. And this sense of possessing a secret gave rise in him to the feeling that he was, in fact, two: "I had found a companion and confidant in myself. There was a secret in this world and it belonged to me and to a somebody who lived in the same body with me. There were two of us, and we could talk with one another" (*Father and Son*, 24). Gosse then goes on to say that some short time later there developed in him a tendency towards the infliction of self-harm, and this:

> culminated in a sort of fit of hysterics, when I lost all self-control, and sobbed with tears, and banged my head on the table. While this was proceeding, I was conscious of that dual individuality of which I have already spoken, since while one part of me gave way, and could not resist, the other part in some extraordinary sense seemed standing aloof, much impressed. (*Ibid.*, 27)

But even if my condition was not unusual, I do not find it surprising that my mother took me, when I was about ten, to see a child psychologist. She told me after the visit that his diagnosis was that

I was a nasty little boy who should learn to control his temper. Years later – I was in my early thirties – she told me that what he had really said was that I was an intelligent and sensitive boy reacting in one normal and expected way to the difficulties of the domestic situation. I do not find it at all puzzling that feelings of guilt pursued me into adulthood and have pervaded my whole life. In any case, my general experience of childhood, as I have said, was of it as a site of violence, which no doubt contributed to my own thought when I was still so young about not having children myself. And looking back, knowing what I now know about H and K, I am sure that I must also have been picking up countless forms of rejection and contempt from those around me. When I learnt years later that my mother had often said to my younger brother, while we were both small boys, that she preferred him to me, I recognized this to be something of the spirit in which she had treated me. I find it impossible to resist the thought that I was treated badly by those around me – I do not mean all the time, and by all those in my life, of course – because I was a child who should never have been there in the first place. A child suffers not simply from being beaten or locked out of the house, as I often was because my mother resorted to such strategies to cope with my temper, but also from the endless infinitely subtle forms of coldness and indifference to which he is prey at the hands of adults. And that such things were there in my young life was in some dim way clear to me even as a child. As I have said, they came, I am sure, from the fact that all those around me knew I was H's son. The adult world was, accordingly, one that I found, for the most part, repellent. Indeed, it engendered in me an intense sense of physical revulsion. Years later, I read Orwell's account of the way in which he felt as a child "cut off from them [adults] by a veil of fear and shyness mixed up with physical disgust". He goes on:

> People are too ready to forget the child's *physical* shrinking from the adult. The enormous size of grown-us, their ungainly,

rigid bodies, their coarse, wrinkled skins, their great relaxed eyelids, their yellow teeth, and the whiffs of musty clothes and beer and sweat and tobacco that disengage from them at every movement! ("Such, Such Were the Joys", 456)

And when I read this passage I felt a strong sense of self-recognition in his physical disgust towards the adult world. This sense of revulsion found in many ways its emblematic moment in an incident that occurred when I was about thirteen or fourteen. K had taken my younger brother and me on a driving holiday around the coast of Scotland. We stopped for the night in a hotel, where the three of us shared a bedroom. At some point in the early hours of the morning I was awakened by an eerie sound as of someone being throttled. K, who was extremely overweight and in the habit of eating a great deal of very rich food, was, I could make out in the pale light coming through the window, standing over the sink and being violently sick; it was clear to me that he had eaten more than his stomach could stand. I was overcome by a sense of revulsion but also, and more distressingly, had the feeling that I was experiencing, there and then, an insight into adult life as being something irredeemably squalid. Despite their countless differences of temperament, something that K and my mother shared was a kind of boundless and largely uncontrollable appetite – in his case for things to eat, in her case for sexual adventure – and it may well be that my image of the squalidness of adult life partly derived from a sense of that life as always balancing precariously on the edge of collapse into self-destructive excess. I suppose that now that I have met H, and have the suspicion that he was probably someone who was rather good at finding ways to thwart or subvert his own pleasure, I have more of an idea why the kind of appetite that K and my mother evinced became for me emblematic of something that makes life unbearable.

To this day the adult world, of which I am now a part, can inspire in me feelings of the kind Orwell describes, many of them self-directed. I do not, however, think I am so unusual in this, although perhaps my response is most recognizable in the fear that we all have of being touched. As Elias Canetti writes:

> There is nothing that man fears more than the touch of the unknown. He wants to *see* what is reaching towards him, and to be able to recognize or at least classify it. Man always tends to avoid physical contact with anything strange … The repugnance to being touched remains with us when we go about among people; the way we move in a busy street, in restaurants, trains or buses, is governed by it. Even when we are standing next to them and are able to watch and examine them closely, we avoid actual contact if we can … The promptness with which apology is offered for an unintentional contact, the tension with which it is awaited, our violent and sometimes even physical reaction when it is not forthcoming, the antipathy and hatred we feel for the offender, even when we cannot be certain who it is … proves that we are dealing with a human propensity as deep-seated as it is alert and insidious; something which never leaves a man when he has once established the boundaries of his personality.
>
> (*Crowds and Power*, 15)

Actually, Orwell makes it clear that his attitude, when a child, towards other boys was not much different from that towards adults, a point he summarily expresses: "[B]oyhood is the age of disgust" ("Such, Such Were the Joys", 439). As a boy, I shared this sense too. Looking back on my childhood, I am aware that I felt extreme fear before many other children, particularly certain boys, and that this had its roots in a conviction that they were physically unclean. This led to an instinctive revulsion at group activities with other children, especially those in an enclosed space, such as Saturday morning cinema, the Christmas pantomime, sports in a gym, sitting on a coach on an outing and so on. Playing sport on a field was fine, because there fresh air was to be found, but I dreaded the communal showers afterwards.

In any case, I suspect that not only is it the case that my sense of domestic life as something violent contributed to my child's thought that I would not have children, but it is also true, I think, that I have sometimes found it hard to believe that any child could not be repelled by me as I was by adults when I was a child. And I strongly suspect that this is one subterranean reason why I have felt unable to have children: I have been incapable of wholly shaking off the thought that they would recoil from me. This is especially so since I am a man: as a child, while I could sometimes find women physically appealing, I always found men physically disgusting. I can think of no man from my childhood to whom I did not react in this way.

The only time having children appeared to me in a different light was in the moment I was told about H: one of my first thoughts was that I must have children, but the thought, or desire – I am not sure which – went almost as quickly, and was replaced by an even stronger sense of not wanting children, since, as I mentioned earlier, I felt polluted and could hardly wish to pass this on.

I sometimes regard my lack of desire to have children as a great loss, a kind of deadness in me. In my middle age I now feel I have to come to terms with it as an absence of desire that I regard as in some way unnatural. I suppose this is because it seems to be not simply that I happen not to want to have children, but that my not wanting them is a kind of moral deformity in me. At any rate, while I do not at all wish to over-romanticize how difficult it is to bring up children, I can see that there is a kind of nobility in doing so. In a way, it is part of (entering) what James Joyce, in his *A Portrait of the Artist as a Young Man*, called "the fair courts of life". Moreover, I see it as an expression of optimism: I think one reason people have children is that, having grasped the compromised nature of life, the desire to start a family is an expression of hope in better things. And beyond that there is something simply extraordinary in someone's being born at all, wondrous in the fact that, as Arendt put it, human parents summon their children into life from the darkness. I think it is, perhaps, in middle age that one first begins to see the nobility and depth of such thoughts. And the reason for this may be that in middle age one begins to understand that the moment when one returns to the darkness oneself is now not so far away: I mean, is no longer a theoretical possibility, but one's inescapable fate, as Tolstoy's Ivan Ilyich suddenly grasps, but seeks to repress.

Ivan Ilych saw that he was dying, and he was in continual despair.

In the depth of his heart he knew he was dying, but so far from growing used to the idea, he simply did not and could not grasp it.

The example of a syllogism which he had learned in Kiesewetter's *Logic*: "Caius is a man, men are mortal, therefore Caius is mortal," had seemed to him all his life to be true as applied to Caius, but certainly not as regards himself. That Caius – man in the abstract – was mortal, was perfectly correct; but he was not Caius, nor man in the abstract: he had always been a creature quite, quite different from all others. He had been little Vanya, with a mamma and a papa, and Mita and Volodya, with playthings and the coachman and nurse; and afterwards with Katya and with all the joys griefs and ecstasies of childhood, boyhood, and youth. What did Caius know of the smell of that striped leather ball Vanya had been so fond of? Was it Caius who had kissed his mother's hand like that, and had Caius heard the silken rustle of her skirts? Was it Caius who had rioted like that over the cakes and pastries at the Law School? Had Caius been in love like that? Could Caius preside at a session as he did?

And Caius was certainly mortal, and it was right for him to die; but for me, little Vanya, Ivan Ilych, with all my thoughts and emotions – it's a different matter altogether. It cannot be that I ought to die. That would be too terrible.

Such was his feeling.

"If I had to die like Caius I should have known it was so, some inner voice would have told me. But there was nothing of the sort in me, and I and all my friends, we knew it was quite different in our case. And now here it is!" he said to himself. "It can't – it can't be, and yet it is! How has it happened? How am I to understand it?"

And he could not understand it, and tried to drive this false, erroneous, morbid thought away and to supplant it with other proper and wholesome thoughts. But the idea, and not the idea only but as it were the reality itself, kept coming back again and confronting him.

(*The Death of Ivan Ilyich*, 137–8)

The wondrous aspect of parents' summoning a child from the darkness is partially reflected in the fact that the child is a wholly animal and spontaneous nature, as a friend of mine said to me shortly after his first child was born. None of the trammels and burdens of self-consciousness interpose themselves between the child and the world. The child is, in a way, looked at from this point of view, still partially in the darkness from which he or she so recently emerged. It is this, I am sure, that partly makes love of a child possible for parents, as my friend suggested to me: the very lack of the child's self-consciousness, his or her wholly innocent and complete existence as nothing more than a body, is central in this love. There is an intense and fragile beauty in the existence of a human being in such a state at the emergence of his or her life. Hence, when I read in the work of some philosophers the claim that what makes a human being the fit object of moral concern is his or her self-consciousness and rationality, and that therefore human infants, possessing neither, are not directly the fit object of such concern, I have the sense that such philosophers understand nothing about life. It is precisely the absence of these in the child that evokes the parents' deepest concern.

Even if it is true that having children is an expression of hope, anyone can see that every child is destined to be confronted with the compromised nature of life, its failures, disappointments, losses and anguish. The hope in question is, however, not, I think, a form of self-deception that things might be otherwise. It is, rather, a kind of affirmation of something about human life; namely, that it is worth living, an affirmation born of, and in the sight of, the intense pleasure that a child can take in life. After all, children, for all that they have their own problems to face, are capable of intense excitement for some of the simplest pleasures of life. They are able to find immense unadulterated joy in life itself, and this is largely because they are able to take such pleasure in their bodies: in running and cycling; in rolling down a hill or throwing themselves into water; in covering themselves in mud or sand; and so on. As I have suggested, adult life, in my view, is in large measure an attempt to find a way back to such moments.

My having no desire to have children can sometimes frighten me, and I take it that many are glad they are parents because they do not have the fear I have, which is not to deny, of course, that they have other anxieties, unknown to me, precisely on account of their having children. I think that ultimately the fear is of something in myself that, as I have said, I find unnatural: a kind of deadness. I feel I do not understand something that others seem to find the most natural desire in the world. And so I feel in a peculiar way cut off from others, as if I lack a certain conception of fellowship with others. It is as though I cannot feel at home in the world, as if I have a sense of myself as so transient as to be unable to get the first foothold in life that could provide me with the means to cement the connection through children. It is some consolation that the authors to whom I feel most drawn – Kafka and Kleist are among the most significant – felt the same way. Strangely, it feels as though I have no connection with history, with the vast teeming masses of humanity connected to the past and the future through their ancestors and descendants. Not all those who do not have children feel this way, I assume; many are perhaps happy in the absence of a desire to have them. But in trying to say why now, in middle age, I am disturbed by my lack of desire here, I have, perhaps, been able to cast a little light on what it is that those in middle age can find consoling in their children.

***

In an interview the philosopher Stanley Cavell offered the following in answer to the question "What does a philosopher do?":

> Of course, the serious answer to that is, they ask themselves that. Almost everybody has his or her own answer to that. All the great philosophers have their answer to it; it winds up in their text, that what they're looking for is a definition of why their lives have been flattened or floored, and how it came to pass that to question themselves was how they wanted to spend their lives. They question themselves and answer themselves in as different ways as there have been the great names in the history of philosophy. I regard myself, and I regard my friends, as trying to find our way among those names.
>
> (*A Philosopher Goes to the Movies*, pt 3)

It will be clear, I think, why I share this sense of philosophy, although Cavell does go on to mention that one can, for different purposes, or in different contexts or moods, give an alternative understanding of what philosophy is – and he is right about that. In fact, most philosophers would be resistant to Cavell's way of understanding philosophy, thinking of it instead as a kind of purely rational, wholly objective and impersonal discipline aimed at finding the one single truth in whichever area the philosopher is exploring, a truth that all would accept if they have followed the philosopher's argument. The mainstream of the subject has conceived of itself in this way ever since Plato invented it. That self-understanding is, in my view, as Nietzsche argued, a falsification that represents, among other things, an anxious desire to take control of the world in thought: in other words, a fantasy of omnipotence in which one leaves behind one's human condition. It is one form of the desire that, Cavell suggests, all human beings have; namely, the longing to escape our condition. No human being, he suggests, is free from the desire to cease being human.

I have tried in this book to think principally about the problematic nature of middle age. In one way, therefore, I have been highlighting some of the temptations to seek to escape what it is to be human. But the very complexities, confusions and unclarities of middle age make available, I think, a view on life that is in some ways affirmative. Arendt drew attention to part of what is at issue here: "Nothing is perhaps more surprising in this world of ours than the almost infinite diversity of its appearances, the sheer entertainment value of its views, sounds, and smells, something that is hardly ever mentioned by the thinkers and philosophers" (*The Life of the Mind*, 20). It belongs to the experience of middle age that one comes to appreciate the force of Arendt's thought: that there is just something amazing at being present – at still being there, despite all the mistakes of the earlier periods of one's life – at such a spectacle. In middle age, precisely because, as Johnson says, we have been able to gain a little distance from a sense of our own importance, we are able to take up, at least at times, a position from which we can value the sheer spectacle of life. And by this I mean the spectacle of both the natural and material world, and the spectacle of human interactions in all their strange and incomprehensible entanglements.

In part, what is at stake here is brought to the fore by the heightened sense in middle age of one's mortality. In an acute discussion of Tolstoy's hatred of Shakespeare, and particularly of *King Lear*, Orwell suggested, in a memorable passage, that:

> what at bottom he [Tolstoy] probably most dislikes [about Shakespeare] is a sort of exuberance, a tendency to take – not so much pleasure, as simply an interest in the actual process of life ... Even the irrelevancies that litter every one of his plays ... are merely the products of excessive vitality. Shakespeare ... loved the surface of the earth and the process of life – which ... is *not* the same thing as wanting to have a good time and stay alive as long as possible.   ("Lear, Tolstoy and the Fool", 413)

In middle age one appreciates properly – or, at any rate, better than at earlier points in one's life – just what it means to affirm life in the kind of way that Orwell suggests Shakespeare was able to. And that is precisely because we know in middle age, as we do not know so clearly at earlier points in life, that we are going to die. Then we know that loving life cannot be a matter of staying alive as long as possible.

I am not claiming, of course, that all those in middle age are able to see their life in this way. It is something that comes to one from time to time if one is lucky: it is no permanent achievement. But it is something, I think, that makes sense as a possibility in middle age, not despite the fact that at this stage in life one is bound to have grasped that life is never what one thought or hoped it would be, but because of this. The absurdities, mistakes, errors, confusions and failures of life, which must strike one in middle age as making up the most part of all that one has done and been, can, at any rate at moments, enable one to have, and no doubt contrary to everything that one would otherwise expect, a heightened sense of why life is worth living at all. There can be a sense of the sheer value of existing at all.

Naturally enough, I am sometimes inclined to think all this nonsense, that youth is right to believe that what makes life worth living could not conceivably be one's mistakes, failures and the rest. It could not be otherwise, if one is honest, than that one is sometimes, perhaps in a way always, tempted to suppose that the young person's view is the right one and that anyone who says otherwise is simply seeking to cover things up. But one knows in middle age that that temptation, while being one whose legitimate rights ought not to be ignored, is also something that cannot possibly open up, and not merely as a form of self-defence, a view on life that even has a hope of capturing it in anything like its further reaches. Middle age is, among other things, an intense negotiation between one's longing for a life complete and lacking in nothing, and the recognition that such a life would, after all, be unbearable.

Afterword

The gods give everything, the infinite ones,
To their beloved, completely,
Every joy, the infinite ones,
Every pain, the infinite ones, completely.

(Goethe, *Selected Poems*, 43)

In his autobiography, *Ecce Homo*, which was written in 1888 but first published in 1908, Nietzsche claims that he had never wasted any time thinking about religious problems and issues such as God, immortality of the soul, redemption, afterlife, guilt, death and so on. In truth, Nietzsche had, in one way or another, spent his life thinking about little else. He says, in a thought to which I have already adverted, that his real concerns were always those of what food to eat, which city or town to live in, what kind of climate was best for him and so on. Nietzsche was less than truthful about the kinds of thoughts to which he had devoted his life because he could see clearly that they had darkened his horizon to no avail: now it was time to put them aside, but he liked to feel that he had never really been bothered by them.

When Nietzsche finished writing his autobiography he was, at the age of forty-four, in a crisis of middle age. He may even have thought he was in late middle age, and that the crisis had been going on for years, since as early as 11 September 1879 he had spoken in a letter to his friend Heinrich Köselitz, who went by the pseudonym of Peter Gast, of his experiencing a breakdown:

I am at the end of my 35th year; the "middle of life" this time has been called for fifteen hundred years. Dante had his vision at this time and speaks of it in the first lines of his poem. Now I am, in the middle of life, so "surrounded by death" that it could seize me at any moment. Given the way I suffer I have to be prepared for a *sudden*, convulsive death (although I would a hundred times prefer a slow, lucid death, during which one could still speak with friends, even if it were more painful). In this way I feel myself to be like the oldest man …

(*Sämtliche Briefe*, vol. 5, 441)

But if Nietzsche wanted to think only of the things that could grace his life and about which he spoke in his work or letters – food, climate, the paintings of Claude, sunlight, fresh water and much else – he also believed that he needed to share them with others properly to do so, as he makes clear in a poem entitled "From High Mountains" appended to his *Beyond Good and Evil*, which was published in 1886:

Oh noontime of life! Time of joy!
    Oh summer garden!
Restless is my happiness as I stand looking and waiting: –
I am waiting for friends, day and night ready,
Where are you, friends? Come! It's time! It's time!
…
Oh noontime of life! Second youth!
    Oh summer garden!
Restless is my happiness as I stand looking and waiting!
I am waiting for friends, day and night ready,
New friends! Come! It's time! It's time!

(*Jenseits von Gut und Böse*, 241, 243)

If Nietzsche had been able to think healthy thoughts and to find the friends he craved, he would at last have found the gentleness and tenderness he had wanted for years. In 1881, in *Daybreak*, he had published a paean to such gentleness in a passage entitled "Where are the needy of spirit?". Nietzsche says that he detests imposing his views on others. Then he goes on:

> [But] there is a still higher festival, when it is for once *allowed* to *give away* one's spiritual house and goods, like a father confessor who sits in the corner, longing for *one who is needy* to come and speak of the troubles in his mind, so that he can fill his hand and heart and make easy his disturbed soul. Not only does he want no fame from this: he would like to avoid gratitude, for this is intrusive and has no shame before loneliness and silence. But to live with no name and gently mocked, too humble to evoke envy or hostility, with a head free of fever, equipped with a handful of knowledge and a sackful of experiences, to be like a poor-doctor of the spirit and to help each and everyone whose head *is disturbed by opinions*, without his even really noticing who has helped him ... Always in a kind of love and always in a kind of self-concern and self-enjoyment! ... That would be a life! That would be a reason to live a long life.   (*Morgenröte*, §449)

And a little later in the book he writes in an even more radiant tone:

> *The ideal selfishness.* – Is there a holier condition than pregnancy? To do everything one does in the calm belief that it must somehow be to the advantage of what is coming to be in us! ... Here one avoids much without having to force oneself to it with difficulty! Here one suppresses a severe word, one offers one's hand in a conciliatory fashion: the child should grow forth from that which is gentlest and best. We shrink

back from our own shrillness and impetuosity: as if this should pour a drop of evil into the cup of life of the dearest unknown person. Everything is veiled, ominous, one has no idea how anything is happening, one waits and seeks to be *prepared.* In this there prevails a pure and purifying feeling of deep unaccountability in us, almost like that had by a spectator before the drawn curtain: *it* is growing, *it* is coming to light: we are in control of nothing, neither its value nor its hour ... – One should live in *this state of consecration!* One can live in this state! Whether that which is expected be a thought, a deed ... This is the genuine *ideal selfishness:* forever to be concerned and to watch and to keep one's soul still that our fruitfulness *may reach maturity beautifully!* Thus, in this direct manner, we care for and watch over the *benefit of all;* and the mood in which we live, this proud and gentle mood, is a balm that spreads itself far around us onto those whose souls are disturbed.   (*Ibid.*, §552)

But Nietzsche was not able to find the gentleness he hoped for and which he felt appropriate to middle age: he lost his mind early in 1889 and spent the rest of his existence in a state of mental eclipse until he died in 1900.

Like Nietzsche, I have spent most of my life thinking about religion and about the kinds of topics I have discussed in this book. And reflecting on Nietzsche's response to his having spent pretty much his whole life thinking about such things, I realize that I too have had my fill of them. For this reason, the moods and feelings of middle age that I describe and seek to understand in this book seem to me, in some ways, to belong to a period of my life that has passed or is passing: although I have striven to be honest in what I have said, I find it hard to recognize myself in some of it.

I think, however, that there is another reason for this. A friend once offered to me in conversation the following thought about the silence of the analyst in psychoanalytic therapy: it is, he reminded me, extraordinarily difficult to remain silent while another talks, but this is the very job of the analyst. And in keeping silent, the analyst allows the client to repeat his own story in such a way that the narrative he offers becomes boring to himself, and he starts to emerge into a different, it is to be hoped more constructive, narrative of his life. While this model of analysis diverges markedly from the practice as it is often understood, it strikes me as insightful and powerful. In a way, I feel that this book is now distant from me for a similar reason: my own story has become boring to me, and this is enabling me to move past it in some ways.

That I feel distanced from my own experiences as I have spoken of them in this book raises once again, in any case, the question of identity – "Who am I?" – that is this book's leading theme and is the principal concern of middle age. The I that speaks in this book is probably less capable than I am in reality of occupying a position between a longing for purity and a sense of disgust or horror with the world or myself. However, to get that into the book would involve rewriting it to such an extent that it would be a different piece of work: hence, I have left the text unchanged. At any rate, I have discussed some of the bleaker aspects of middle age, and I know I am far from being alone in finding much that is pretty barren in middle age, but I would not wish to suggest that there is nothing especially good about this time of life, and here and there I have sought to suggest what that might be.

A colleague of mine recently remarked to me that one of the good things about middle age for him was his having secured a place in his chosen career that means that he no longer has to struggle to establish himself and worry about whether he ever will. He is right about this, and I consider myself extremely lucky to be at a point in life where I have a place in a career that I long wanted. Moreover, I think that whatever talents I might have are well rewarded by teaching and writing, although I do not mean this in terms of material gain – not that I would want to complain at all about that side of things. Further, I feel generally extremely fortunate to be alive in present society, which, despite its endless idiocies, has provided me with opportunities that, had I been born in pretty much any other time, I would not have had: in just about no other age could someone from my social and cultural background have had the chance for an education of the quality that I was privileged to receive, and for this I have to thank the liberal, egalitarian aspirations of the modern age. I think I am probably able to appreciate this properly for the first time in middle age.

It goes without saying that none of this precludes my seeing the absurdities and injustices of the world, but I suppose that middle age has given me the hope that I might be at least a little less disposed than I once was of reading any personal difficulties I have into an account of what is wrong with the world. Nothing is more common than that we project our personal dissatisfactions onto the world at large in a way that means we fail to see exactly what those problems are and what is wrong with the world. I am just as prey to doing this as anyone else, indeed, probably more so, since part of my profession is to spend a great deal of time thinking, which is likely to lead to dissatisfaction since thought is in many ways largely self-destructive. But I think middle age is at least a moment of hope that it is possible to gain a modicum of distance here since, if we have been lucky, we have found by then a place in life that, materially speaking, allows us to do a fair bit of what we want to do.

But supposing that middle age brings with it this kind of solution to what D. H. Lawrence called "the bread-and-butter problem of alimentation" (*Fantasia of the Unconscious*, 254) and some space in which to pursue the things one values and be who one wants to be, there still remains the problem that, as Rowan Williams puts it: "letting our best-loved pictures of ourselves and our achievements die, trying to live without the protections we are used to, *feels* like hell, most of the time. But the real hell is never to be able to rest from the labours of self-defence" (*Silence and Honeycakes*, 48). Perhaps middle age is a rare gift because one has the time then to try to rest from such labours.

One way, I think, of capturing this is in terms of the kind of scepticism I have previously mentioned. Scepticism as a philosophical school or style of thought goes back to at least the fourth century BCE. In one central form it argues, roughly speaking, that each philosophical argument for a given conclusion can be opposed by an equally convincing argument for the diametrically opposed conclusion. Philosophy cannot establish knowledge on this view. A variant on, or form of, this outlook is the claim that reason can be shown to undermine itself and is thus incapable of providing knowledge, and philosophers have been grappling with the problem in this form since at least the middle of the eighteenth century. In my view, the history of Western philosophy shows the impotence of reason and its incapacity to establish any definitive conclusions: reason is, in fact, self-undermining. Despite all the efforts of philosophers and other thinkers, no one in fact knows, for example, if there is a God or even how we should best conceive what it would be for God to exist; or what, exactly, free will is, and whether we have it; whether evil exists, and if so, what its nature is; what the point and purpose of art is; and so on. It may, of course, be a matter of temperament, but I am myself not unduly bothered by any of this. Quite the contrary: as I said earlier, I find it offers a certain kind of freedom. In a way, my trajectory towards a philosophical scepticism and the development and nature of my personal experiences have met at this point in my life, in early middle age: both intimate the same sense of a kind of distance from life, a willingness not to expect too much, which I find I am able sometimes to mobilize to give me some sense of calm that I think I would not otherwise have had. I do not want to exaggerate: I can only marshal my energies in this way intermittently and very imperfectly, but when I do, however poorly, I can see why the ancient sceptics thought that scepticism provided *ataraxia*, tranquillity.

There is a connection here with two ideas, both found in Christian thought, but not only there. The first is suggested by Williams, when he writes that the "'world' is a place where it is barely possible to speak without making things more difficult and destructive" (*Silence and Honeycakes*, 70). Williams suggests that a constructive response to this is silence. He does not mean that one should say nothing, of course. He speaks rather of an *"expectant quiet"*. He means, I take it, in part, that one should *take one's time*, and I think here of Wittgenstein's suggestion that when philosophers meet they should greet each other with this salutation: "Take your time" (*Culture and Value*, 80). But, in a way, that is how we should all greet each other when we meet. Taking one's time, or being silent in the sense in question, is a matter of acting on one's reminder to oneself that one knows hardly anything and is profoundly fallible. It is also a way of reminding oneself of the point I made earlier that in any conversation it is a serious question what one would achieve in convincing others of one's own view. The answer is usually: next to nothing.

All this is related to the second idea connected with the hope for tranquillity I am discussing: waiting. By middle age most people grasp, I think, how little one can get of what really matters in life by doing anything other than waiting for it. Friendship and love are two key examples, in which the effort to get what one wants will nearly always lead to its destruction. The kind of distance I mentioned as being characteristic of philosophical scepticism and of the experiences one is likely to have had by middle age nourishes the ability to wait, which, I am suggesting, helps with achieving at least a modicum of inner calm. When Thomas Mann's Gustav Aschenbach, the writer-hero of his *Death in Venice*, becomes ill at the age of fifty-two, one of those who has seen him says: "'Look, Aschenbach has always lived like this' – and the speaker closed the fingers of his left hand tight into a fist – ; 'never in this way' – and he let his opened hand dangle comfortably over the side of the armchair" (*Der Tod in Venedig*, 193). Being able to wait is rather like allowing one's hand to hang in this way. Middle age has given me something of the ability so to live, and for this reason I find it in certain respects a better time of life than others. Perhaps I am not alone in having this experience in mid-life.

When I think about it I find it odd that H and K were about my age when H had the affair with my mother. I find H and K less alien in their behaviour because of this. In a way, it all seems so long ago that the pain and suffering they all caused each other hardly matters now, I suppose. After all, I know that H's wife knew of the affair, although not of me, of course, and forgave him. H told me that when K confronted him about the affair he, H, felt deep shame because K treated him in such a gentlemanly way (that was his word). It seemed to him to make it all worse. And K obviously did his best to make the situation tenable in taking me on as his son. I am reminded here of a passage in Theodor Fontane's *Effi Briest*. Innstetten has found out that, years ago, his wife had an affair. He says to a friend:

> The fact is I'm unspeakably unhappy; I have been insulted, shamelessly deceived – but yet I have no feeling of hatred or even thirst for revenge. And when I ask myself, why not?, I can find no other explanation than the years that have passed. Everyone talks about unforgivable guilt: there's clearly no such thing for God, but for people too. I would never have believed that *time*, simply time as such, could have such an effect.
>
> (*Effi Briest*, 235)

All lives contain suffering in one form or another; that is just the human condition. Part of the shape it took in the lives of H, K and my mother was the affair: betrayal, deception, lies, guilt, fear and the rest. One is tempted to say that, had it not taken this form, it would have taken another, and I am sure that if one is able to see one's life in such terms then the suffering in it seems somehow less awful or unmanageable. But it will be, among other things, the passage of time that makes this a possibility, I think, as Fontane saw. I certainly fairly often see my own life in this way, which is only possible because enough time has passed for me to do so, in which case there is something consoling about being in middle age. In an odd way, I sometimes see what I have found out about myself as a kind of strange privilege, affording me insights into things that would otherwise have remained closed. Yet in truth I do not understand who I am, and I think I never will, and that can be a disorientating thought. But in this respect I am, after all, just like everyone else.

A final thought

Men must endure
Their going hence even as their coming hither.
Ripeness is all.   (Shakespeare, *King Lear* V.ii.9–11)

Just as I finished the manuscript of this book and was about to send
it to the publisher, H died. I had visited him about four days before.
It is too early for me to be clear what exactly H's death means to me.
I certainly regret the fact that I came to know him so late in his life,
when he was already very frail, that it was not possible to forge a
proper relationship with him. But when I reflect that he might easily
already have been dead when I found out about him I am pleased
to have had the chance to meet him at all.

In the last five years I saw H about seven or eight times, sometimes in the company of my siblings from H's wife, who have been
extremely kind to me and to whom I am profoundly grateful for
their warmth. I do not know whether I might have wanted to see
him more often, but he emphasized when we first spoke that he
did not want his life to be changed in any way by my appearing in
his life and was obviously frightened at the thought that I might
want him to have something to do with my Hamilton siblings or
my mother. He need not have worried, since that was the last thing
on my mind.

Apart from the first time I saw H, our conversations always
turned around everyday matters concerning the things we had
been doing. But on that first occasion we spoke intimately, partly

because I felt I had the right to ask questions of him that one would not normally ask of one's parents. The relationship I had with him was thus odd: at once much less intimate than people normally have with their parents, with whom they share much of their life, and also much more intimate. I very much felt the strangeness of my relationship with him the first time I met him when, at one point during our conversation, he stood up and said that he would make a cup of tea. "You don't mind if your old dad makes you some tea, do you?", he asked, and patted me on the back. I could not think of him as my "old dad" and felt the moment to be unreal, even uncanny: I knew why he said what he said, and I knew it was meant affectionately, but it made me feel as if K were being usurped in my life and as if I ought to feel a warmth for H I could not muster.

In a peculiar way, and despite the oddity of my relationship with H, his death leaves me with a sense that most have, I think, when their parents die; namely, the feeling that somehow a connection with the world has gone, a certain kind of rootedness or background. The feeling is one of a weird loneliness. What is strange is that H was not even in the most attenuated sense able to provide for me a concrete or practical connection with the world. My sense, then, of the connection he provided is very largely a matter of my being of his flesh and blood, of the sheer unfathomable fact that he was my biological father: unfathomable as such a fact always is for anyone, since it is always in various ways odd that *this* person is one's father, *this* one's mother, but perhaps especially so for me because this man was my former teacher, itself a relationship at once intimate and very distant. It was like being told that that stranger – that old man in the cafe over there, as it may be – is one's father, and yet not like that at all, because I already knew H. Finding out that he was my father was thus even more uncanny than being told that a stranger was my father. In the end, the oddity was simply the strangeness of the unique situation it was, and yet it was in many ways just like that which anyone faces in his or her parents, as I have tried to bring out in this book.

Because I have had two fathers, I have no real idea who my father is. Yet that, too, is not so unusual, since many feel that, in middle age, they grasp that they have no idea who their parents are: they have known them as providers in various ways, but suddenly they are seen as adults in their own right, with their own needs and desires that one must get to know. This may, but need not, be because, when people are in middle age, their parents are likely to be entering a period of life when they increasingly need the support of their children in various ways.

In thinking about H's death, I am struck by the feeling, typical for such a situation, that I can hardly believe he is dead, that his unique perspective on the world, the perspective that he *was*, is gone. Yet I feel none of the grief that a son might feel at losing his father, which I am sure is only to be expected given the peculiarities of my relationship with him. Perhaps it is because he appeared out of the blue in my life some six years ago and now has disappeared from it just as suddenly that I have a most peculiar feeling that he never really existed, or, perhaps better, never really existed as my father. I feel almost as if my connection with him was a mere dream or hallucination, and that this state has come to an end. It is also for me as if I am now in a dream, and I feel somewhat light-headed at the thought that he is dead. It is as if I have been released, but it is unclear into what I have been released. Certainly it is not into the state I was in before I found out about him. But oddly, I have much the same feeling now as I had when I first was told that H was my father: a kind of sense that my life lies in others' hands. Perhaps that is a common feeling when a parent dies: something profound for one's own life happens that is in fact, so to speak, an event in the life of another. I suppose it is a matter of recognizing one's profound dependence on others regardless of whether one wants this. For me this involves an eerie but calm feeling as if something significant but unknown is preparing itself in me; hence the sense of being in a dreamlike state.

It may seem peculiar to say this, but there is a way in which I feel H's death to be a kind of betrayal, as if he had no right to appear in my life and then withdraw in this way. No doubt that is a form of unthinking, instinctive egoism on my part. In any case, the feeling of being betrayed is, of course, always a demand for fidelity, which is itself a form of possessiveness and so egoism, although it is an egoism that can be welcomed by the person on whom the demand is made, not least because it can be pleasing to be needed or possessed. But in another way it makes no sense, of course, for me to feel betrayed by H, since there is no way in which he exercised any choice when his life came to an end. It is true that we can feel that others have to answer for their actions even when they had no choice in doing what they did: Oedipus felt himself responsible for killing his father and marrying his mother even though he could not have done otherwise. But when it is a question of someone's dying then, aside from cases such as suicide, the idea of his or her being responsible has no place. After all, we are dealing here with an absolute limit to the human condition. Nonetheless, the feeling of betrayal remains, beyond all reason and judgement, as if the condition of one's own existence cannot himself cease to exist. I suppose that is part of the reason why even more acutely than before I feel surrounded by death on all sides.

In a way, what I feel now that H is gone is an even sharper sense of the force of the question: what was it all for? Of course, as I said at the outset of this book, I was told about H by one of my brothers, but it is as if H turned up in my life, creating havoc and chaos, and then left just as abruptly. What on earth was the point of it all? I wonder if my feelings here are largely misdirected. H, after all, when he was my teacher, did not know I was his son. Yet my mother said to me that she once told him about me. She is such an unreliable source of information that I have no idea whether to believe her or not. Nonetheless, I find it hard to think that H did not suspect I was his son – after all, it must have been clear to him that I was born at a time that made it possible for him to be my father – but I can understand why he would not have wanted to probe the issue deeply. So my anger, if that is what it is, that he appeared in my life and then disappeared again perhaps has some justification. If he had suspicions, did he just hope I would never have them too? And again, my older Hamilton brothers and sister knew all along, and kept things from me. I know they did this in the belief it was for the best, but one of them recently telephoned me to apologise: it now strikes him, he said, as utterly incredible that they all thought they had some right to conceal from me who my father was. And further, he went on to say, he now realized that when they told me it was too late for me to establish a proper relationship with him, which only made everything worse. His apology moved me, and I was, and am, extremely grateful for it.

One thing that has struck me in all this is that very few people seem to have much understanding of why it is that my life was undermined so profoundly by my finding out that H was my father. Perhaps it is one of those things that you cannot understand unless you have experienced it for yourself. Or perhaps many people do not want to understand: it touches so deeply problems about identity that we all have. But often I have had the feeling that some of those around me simply wanted to pretend that nothing was changed by the revelation: and for some, such as all but one of my Hamilton siblings, nothing did change, since they had known most of my life anyway. That may have made it more difficult for them to grasp what it all meant, and means, to me, although perhaps all the more urgent for them to try.

Beyond everything else, this remains: I have two fathers, both dead now, and one mother with whom it is impossible for me to have a decent relationship. I have six half-brothers and two half-sisters. I am Christopher Hamilton, and I am someone else whose identity remains a mystery to me. My life has woven into it, and at its deepest level, lies and deceit, mendacity and deception. I struggle to make sense of all this, but eventually I always return, in bleak moments, to the thought that all that is self-deception, because in the end there is no meaning to be found in any of it.

Bibliography

Adorno, T. 1987. *Minima Moralia: Reflections from Damaged Life*, E. F. N. Jephcott (trans.). London: Verso.

Améry, J. 1994. *On Ageing*, J. D. Barlow (trans.). Bloomington, IN: Indiana University Press.

Arendt, H. 1958. *The Human Condition*. Chicago, IL: University of Chicago Press.

Arendt, H. 1971. *The Life of the Mind*. New York: Harcourt Brace.

Arendt, H. 1983. "On Humanity in Dark Times". In *Men in Dark Times*, 3–31. New York: Harcourt Brace.

Auden, W. H. 1968. *Secondary Worlds*. London: Faber.

Bachmann, I. 2007. "Das dreißigste Jahr". In *Das dreißigste Jahr: Erzählungen*, 17–60. Munich/Zurich: Piper. Published in English as *The Thirtieth Year: Stories*, M. Bullock (trans.) (Teaneck, NJ: Holmes & Meier, 1995).

Bate, W. J. 1984. *Samuel Johnson*. London: Hogarth Press.

Berthoud, J. 1978. *Joseph Conrad: The Major Phase*. Cambridge: Cambridge University Press.

Büchner, G. 1994. *Leonce und Lena*. In *Werke und Briefe*, 159–89. Munich: Deutscher Taschenbuch. Published in English in *Complete Plays, "Lenz" and Other Writings*, J. Reddick (trans.) (Harmondsworth: Penguin, 1993).

Camus, A. 2006. *Le Mythe de Sisyphe*. Paris: Gallimard. Published in English as *The Myth of Sisyphus*, J. O'Brien (trans.) (Harmondsworth: Penguin, 1981).

Canetti, E. 1973. *Crowds and Power*, C. Stewart (trans.). Harmondsworth: Penguin.

Cavell, S. 2002. *A Philosopher Goes to the Movies*. http://globetrotter.berkeley.edu/people2/Cavell/cavell-con0.html [accessed Jan. 2009].

Chekov, A. 1987. "A Boring Story". In *Lady With Lapdog and Other Stories*, D. Magarshack (trans.), 46–104. Harmondsworth: Penguin.

Chesterton, G. K. 2004. *Orthodoxy*. New York: Dover.

Conrad, J. 1928. *Letters from Conrad 1895–1924*, E. Garnett (ed.). London: Nonesuch Press.

Conrad, J. 1983. *Lord Jim*, J. Batchelor (ed.). Oxford: Oxford University Press.

Conrad, J. 1989. *Nostromo*, K. Carabine (ed.). Oxford: Oxford University Press.

Critchley, S. 2007. *On Humour*. London: Routledge.

Deschavanne, É. & P.-H. Tavoillot 2007. *Philosophie des âges de la vie*. Paris: Hachette.

Eliot, T. S. 1986. *Collected Poems 1909–1962*. London: Faber.

Fingarette, H. 1997. *Death: Philosophical Soundings*. Chicago, IL: Open Court.

Fontane, T. 1992. *Effi Briest*. Frankfurt: Ullstein. Published in English as *Effi Briest*, H. Rorrison & H. Chambers (trans.) (Harmondsworth: Penguin, 1995).

Gaita, R. 2003. *The Philosopher's Dog*. London: Routledge.

Genet, J. 2001. "Ce qui est resté d'un Rembrandt déchiré en petits carrés bien réguliers, et foutu aux chiottes". In *Oeuvres Complètes*, vol. IV, 19–31. Paris: Gallimard.

Genet, J. 2003. "Rembrandt's Secret". In *Fragments of the Artwork*, C. Mandell (trans.), 84–90. Stanford, CA: Stanford University Press.

Goethe, J. W. von 1972. *Selected Poems*, B. Fairley (ed.). London: Heinemann.

Goethe, J. W. von n.d., *Aus meinem Leben: Dichtung und Wahrheit*, http://www.odysseetheater.com/goethe/duw/duw00.htm [accessed January 2009]. Published in English as *From my Own Life: Poetry and Truth*, J. Oxenford (trans.) (Kila, MT: Kessinger, 2007).

Gorky, M. 1999. *Summerfolk*, V. Liber (trans.), version N. Dear. London: Faber.

Gosse, E. 2004. *Father and Son*, M. Newton (ed.). Oxford: Oxford University Press.

Hofmannsthal, H. von 1902. *Brief des Lord Chandos an Francis Bacon*, http://gutenberg.spiegel.de/?id=5&xid=1247&kapitel=1#gb_found [accessed January 2009]. Published in English as *The Lord Chandos Letter*, J. Rotenberg (trans.) (New York: New York Review of Books, 2007).

Hopkins, G. M. 1976. *Poems and Prose*, W. H. Gardner (ed.). Harmondsworth: Penguin.

Jaques, E. 1965. "Death and the Mid-Life Crisis". *International Journal of Psychoanalysis* **46**: 502–24.

Kafka, F. 2006. *Die Zürauer Aphorismen*. Frankfurt: Suhrkamp. Published in English as *Zürau Aphorisms*, M. Hofmann, R. Calasso & G. Brock (trans.) (London: Harvill Secker, 2006).

Kant, I. 2001. *Lectures on Ethics*, P. Heath (trans.). Cambridge: Cambridge University Press.

Kass, L. 1999. *The Hungry Soul*. Chicago, IL: University of Chicago Press.

Kierkegaard, S. 1978. *Journals and Papers: Vol. I*, E. H. Hong & H. V. Hong (trans.). Bloomington, IN: Indiana University Press.

Kuhn, R. 1976. *The Demon of Noontide: Ennui in Western Literature*. Princeton, NJ: Princeton University Press.

Larkin, P. 1974. *High Windows*. London: Faber.

Larkin, P. 1990. *Collected Poems*. London: Faber.

Larkin, P. 2002. *Further Requirements: Interviews, Broadcasts, Statements and Book Reviews 1952–1985*, A. Thwaite (ed.). London: Faber.

Lawrence, D. H. 1971. *Fantasia of the Unconscious: Psychoanalysis and the Unconscious*. Harmondsworth: Penguin.

MacDonald, I. 2005. *Revolution in the Head*. London: Pimlico.

Machiavelli, N. 2002. *The Prince*, R. Price (trans.). Cambridge, Cambridge University Press.

Mann, T. 1995. *Der Tod in Vendig* in *Schwere Stunde und andere Erzählungen*. Frankfurt: Fischer. Published in English as *Death in Venice* in *Death in Venice. Tristan. Tonio Kröger*, H. T. Lowe-Porter (trans.) (Harmondsworth: Penguin, 1955).

Maugham, W. S. 1944. *The Summing-Up*. London: Heinemann.

Mill, J. S. 1971. *Mill on Bentham and Coleridge*, F. R. Leavis (intro.). London: Chatto & Windus.

Mitchell, J. 1996. *Joe Gould's Secret*. New York: Modern Library.

Montaigne, M. de 1991. *The Complete Essays*, M. Screech (trans.). Harmondsworth: Penguin.

Murdoch, I. 1986. *The Sovereignty of Good*. London: Ark.

Musil, R. 1994. *Der Mann ohne Eigenschaften: Erstes und Zweites Buch*. Hamburg: Rowohlt. Published in English as *The Man Without Qualities*, S. Wilkins & B. Pike (trans.) (New York: Picador, 1997).

Nagel, T. 1985. *The View from Nowhere*. New York: Oxford University Press.

Nietzsche, F. 1986. *Sämtliche Briefe Nietzsches* (Complete letters). In *Kritische Studienausgabe, 8 Bände*, vol. 5, G. Colli & M. Montinari (eds). Berlin: de Gruyter.

Nietzsche, F. 1988. *Die fröhliche Wissenschaft*. In *Kritische Studienausgabe in 15 Bänden*, vol. 3, G. Colli & M. Montinari (eds), 343–651. Berlin: de Gruyter. Published in English as *The Gay Science*, W. Kaufmann (trans.) (New York: Random House, 1991).

Nietzsche, F. 1988. *Morgenröte*. In *Kritische Studienausgabe in 15 Bänden*, vol. 3, G. Colli & M. Montinari (eds), 9–331. Berlin: de Gruyter. Published in English as *Daybreak*, R. J. Hollingdale (trans.) (Cambridge: Cambridge University Press, 1982).

Nietzsche, F. 1988. *Jenseits von Gut und Böse*. In *Kritische Studienausgabe in 15 Bänden*, vol. 5, G. Colli & M. Montinari (eds), 9–243. Berlin: de Gruyter. Published in English as *Beyond Good and Evil*, R. J. Hollingdale (trans.) (Harmondsworth: Penguin, 1990).

Nietzsche, F. 1988. *Ecce Homo*. In *Kritische Studienausgabe in 15 Bänden*, vol. 6, G. Colli & M. Montinari (eds), 255–374. Berlin: de Gruyter. Published in English as *Ecce Homo*, R. J. Hollingdale (trans.) (Harmondsworth: Penguin, 1988).

Oakeshott, M. 1991. "The Voice of Poetry in the Conversation of Mankind". In his *Rationalism in Politics and Other Essays*, 488–541. Indianapolis, IN: Liberty Fund.

Orwell, G. 1984. "Such, Such Were the Joys". In *The Penguin Essays of George Orwell*, 422–58. Harmondsworth: Penguin.

Orwell, G. 1984. "Lear, Tolstoy and the Fool". In *The Penguin Essays of George Orwell*, 407–22. Harmondsworth: Penguin.

Phillips, A. 1994. *On Kissing, Tickling and Being Bored*. London: Faber.

Phillips, A. 2006. *Going Sane*. Harmondsworth: Penguin.

Ricks, C. 1995. *Beckett's Dying Words*. Oxford: Oxford University Press.

Rilke, R. M. 1982. *Die Aufzeichnungen des Malte Laurids Brigge*. Frankfurt: Insel.

Published in English as *The Notebooks of Malte Laurids Brigge*, S. Mitchell (trans.) (New York: Random House, 1990).

Rilke, R. M. *Duineser Elegien* http://gutenberg.spiegel.de/?id=5&xid=2251&kapite l=1#gb_found [accessed January 2009]. Published in English as *Duino Elegies*, J. B. Leishmann & S. Spender (trans.) (London: Hogarth Press, 1963).

Rochefoucauld, F. de la 1977. *Maximes*. Paris: Flammarion. Published in English as *Maxims*, L. W. Tancock (trans.) (Harmondsworth: Penguin, 1959).

Russell, B. 1995. *Portraits from Memory*. Nottingham: Spokesman Books.

Sebald, W. G. 2003. *Austerlitz*. Frankfurt: Fischer. Published in English as *Austerlitz*, A. Bell (trans.) (Harmondsworth: Penguin, 1959).

Shklar, J. 1998. *Political Thought and Political Thinkers*. Chicago, IL: University of Chicago Press.

Steiner, G. 1998. "Tragedy, Pure and Simple". In *Tragedy and the Tragic: Greek Theatre and Beyond*, M. S. Silk (ed.), 534–46. Oxford: Clarendon Press.

Stern, J. P. 1964. *Re-Interpretations: Seven Studies in Nineteenth-Century German Literature*. London: Thames & Hudson.

Stifter, A. 1991. "Brigitta". In his *Erzählungen*, 19–85. Frankfurt: Insel. Published in English as "Brigitta", in *"Brigitta" and Other Tales*, H. Watanabe-O'Kelly (trans.) (Harmondsworth: Penguin, 1994).

Tolstoy, L. 1960. *The Death of Ivan Ilych and Other Stories*, R. Edmonds (trans.). Harmondsworth: Penguin.

Tolstoy, L. 1980. *Anna Karenina*, L. Maude & A. Maude (trans.). Oxford: Oxford University Press.

Tolstoy, L. 1987. *A Confession and Other Religious Writings*, J. Kentish (trans.). Harmondsworth: Penguin.

Weil, S. 1957. "Luttons-nous pour la justice?". In her *Écrits de Londres et dernières letters*, 45–57. Paris: Gallimard. Published in English as "Are We Struggling for Justice?", M. Barabas (trans.), *Philosophical Investigations* **10**(1) (1987): 1–10.

Williams, R. 2003. *Silence and Honeycakes*. Oxford: Lion Hudson.

Wittgenstein, L. 1986. *Philosophical Investigations*, G. E. M. Anscombe (trans.). Oxford: Blackwell.

Wittgenstein, L. 1992. *Culture and Value*, P. Winch (trans.). Oxford: Blackwell.

Wollheim, R. 2005. *Germs: A Memoir of Childhood*. London: Black Swan.

Woolf, V. 2002. *On Being Ill*. Ashfield, MA: Paris Press.

Wordsworth, W. 1974. Preface to *Lyrical Ballads*. In *English Critical Texts*, D. J. Enright & E. de Chickera (eds). Oxford: Oxford University Press.

Zweig, S. 1999. *Drei Meister: Balzac. Dickens. Dostojewski*. Frankfurt: Fischer.

Zweig, S. 2003. *Montaigne*. Frankfurt: Fischer.

Index

Heidegger, M. 16, 64
Hofmannsthal, H. von 17
Hopkins, G. M. 34
humour 88; *see also* comedy

illness 7, 40
independence 35–6

Jaques, E. 70
Johnson, S. 23–4, 25–6, 30, 87, 91,
    92, 104
Joyce, J. 99

Kafka, F. 83, 103
Kant, I. 74
Kass, L. 92, 93, 94
Keats, J. 12
Kierkegaard, S. 45
Kleist, H. von 103
Kuhn, R. 60

language 17–19, 24, 56
Laplanche, J. 88
Larkin, P. 15, 33, 41
Lawrence, D. H. 112
Leavis, F. R. 26
Lennon, J. 48
loneliness 21, 24–5, 31, 35–6, 118
loss, sense of 50
love 3–6, 20, 24–5, 35–6, 45, 69

MacDonald, I. 48
Machiavelli, N. 22
Mann, T. 114
manner 35, 89
marriage 24, 25
Maugham, W. S. 15
McEwan, I. 8
memory 53–5
Mill, J. S. 80, 84
Mitchell, J. 51
Montaigne, M. 88–91, 93–4
Moon, K. 48
morality 13, 23, 66, 71

mortality 8, 9, 48, 105; *see also*
    death
Murdoch, I. 68
music 50
Musil, R. 27–8
mystery 4, 34

Nagel, T. 31–2
names 32–4, 35
Nietzsche, F. 12, 17, 30, 66, 81–3,
    86, 104, 107–10
nostalgia 49–53, 57, 59

Oakeshott, M. 92, 93, 94
Orwell, G. 46, 66, 96–8, 105

pain 11
Pascal, B. 62
Paul 83
personality *see* character
personal identity 59–60
Phillips, A. 72, 88
philosophy, nature of xi–xii, 23,
    103–4
place, sense of 57–9
Plato 104
play 91–3
pleasure 30–31, 83–6, 102
pollution 6, 9
Proust, M. 57–8, 70–71
psychoanalysis 111
purity 47, 49
    longing for 24–5, 70, 111

Rembrandt 46–9
Ricks, C. 78–9
Rilke, R. M. 10, 66
Russell, B. 19

scepticism 30, 94, 113–14
Schnitzler, A. 74
Schopenhauer, A. 14, 77–8
Sebald, W. G. 48, 49
sex(ual desire) 34, 37–9